ITALIAN
GARDENS

ACKNOWLEDGEMENTS

Our grateful thanks are due to all those garden owners and gardeners whose loving labours have created and preserved the gardens of Italy. So many owners have been helpful to us that they cannot all be mentioned. Our thanks to them all, most particularly for their generosity in making their gardens accessible to visitors.

Many public officials and organisations were most generous with time and information. Among them we would like to thank: Dr Renata Lodari (Consigliere del Museo di Verbania), Dr Paolo Odone (Direttore Servizio Giardini, Turin), Dr Pellizon and Dr Zago (Regione del Veneto), Dr Giancarlo della Santa (Segretario Regionale 'Agriturist', Florence), and the staff of the Ente di Turismo, Salerno. We would also like to thank the authorities at the Quirinal gardens for their interest and assistance.

Our labours were considerably lightened by the support and encouragement of our friends. Much as we'd like to, we can't mention everyone. However we would like to record our gratitude to all those with whom we stayed on our many journeys. Our thanks to Luigina Benci, Sulie and François Bruzzi, Stefanella Griccioli, Anne and Giovanni Grotanelli, and Piera and Annibale Osti. Our especial thanks to Valeria Grilli, whose kindness to us and to our riotous year–old daughter rose far above the call of friendship.

Cover photo: Villa Arrighetti, Tuscany
Opposite: La Mortola, Liguria

ITALIAN GARDENS

A VISITOR'S GUIDE

ALEX RAMSAY and HELENA ATTLEE

Edited by David Joyce

Robertson McCarta

First published in 1989 by

Robertson McCarta Limited
122 Kings Cross Road
London WC1X 9DS

Managing Editor Folly Marland
Designed by Christine Wood
Production by Grahame Griffiths
Typeset by Book Ens, Saffron Walden, Essex
Printed and bound in Italy by Grafedit S.P.A. Bergamo

British Library Cataloguing in Publication Data

Attlee, Helena, 1958–
    Italian gardens: a guide for visitors.
    1. Italy. Gardens. Visitors' guides
    I. Title   II. Ramsay, Alex, 1950–
    914.5'04928

    ISBN 1-85365-182-6

CONTENTS

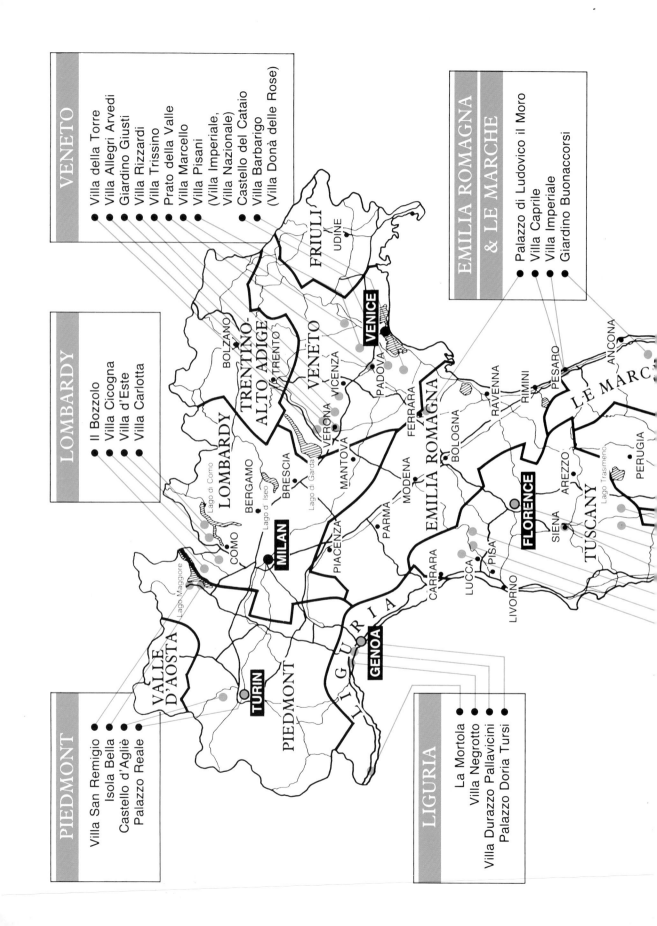

VENETO

- Villa della Torre
- Villa Allegri Arvedi
- Giardino Giusti
- Villa Rizzardi
- Villa Trissino
- Prato della Valle
- Villa Marcello
- Villa Pisani
- (Villa Imperiale, Villa Nazionale)
- Castello del Cataio
- Villa Barbarigo (Villa Donà delle Rose)

LOMBARDY

- Il Bozzolo
- Villa Cicogna
- Villa d'Este
- Villa Carlotta

PIEDMONT

- Villa San Remigio
- Isola Bella
- Castello d'Agliè
- Palazzo Reale

EMILIA ROMAGNA & LE MARCHE

- Palazzo di Ludovico il Moro
- Villa Caprile
- Villa Imperiale
- Giardino Buonaccorsi

LIGURIA

- La Mortola
- Villa Negrotto
- Villa Durazzo Pallavicini
- Palazzo Doria Tursi

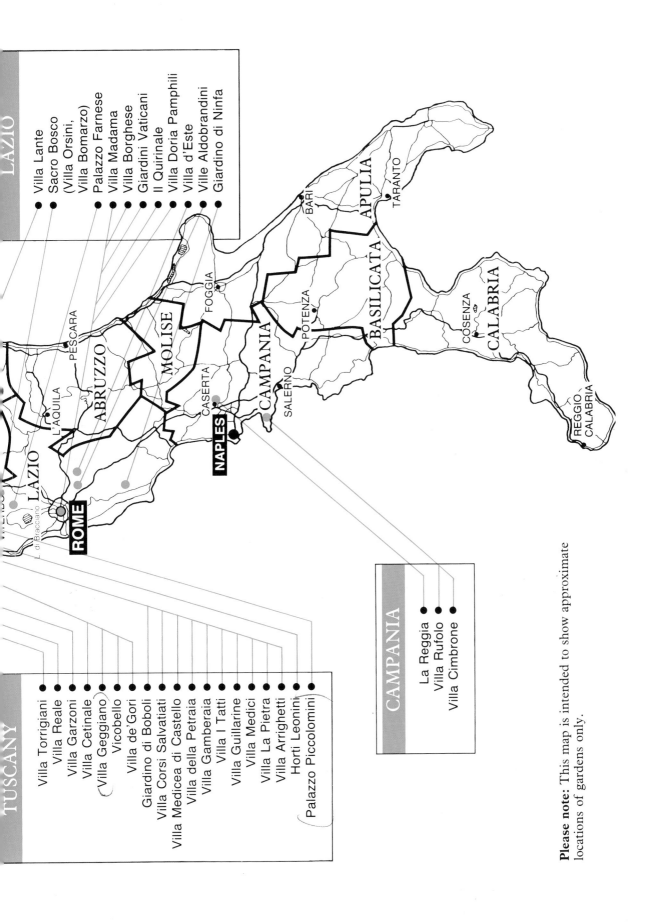

Please note: This map is intended to show approximate locations of gardens only.

LAZIO

- Villa Lante
- Sacro Bosco (Villa Orsini, Villa Bomarzo)
- Palazzo Farnese
- Villa Madama
- Villa Borghese
- Giardini Vaticani
- Il Quirinale
- Villa Doria Pamphili
- Villa d'Este
- Ville Aldobrandini
- Giardino di Ninfa

TUSCANY

- Villa Torrigiani
- Villa Reale
- Villa Garzoni
- Villa Cetinale
- Villa Geggiano
- Vicobello
- Villa de'Gori
- Giardino di Boboli
- Villa Corsi Salvatiati
- Villa Medicea di Castello
- Villa della Petraia
- Villa Gamberaia
- Villa I Tatti
- Villa Guillarine
- Villa Medici
- Villa La Pietra
- Villa Arrighetti
- Horti Leonini
- Palazzo Piccolomini

CAMPANIA

- La Reggia
- Villa Rufolo
- Villa Cimbrone

ABRUZZO

MOLISE

APULIA

BASILICATA

CALABRIA

CAMPANIA

PESCARA

L'AQUILA

FOGGIA

CASERTA

NAPLES

SALERNO

POTENZA

BARI

TARANTO

COSENZA

REGGIO CALABRIA

ROME

L. di Bracciano

INTRODUCTION

For centuries travellers have been drawn to the gardens of Italy. Their admiration and astonishment fill the pages of countless letters and diaries. Anyone willing to leave the well-trodden paths of tourism and seek out the lesser known gardens in this book will find them still as compellingly beautiful. The dark green of cypress and yew, black shadows, pale statues and shimmering pools leave a lasting impression on the imagination.

Before its unification in 1860 Italy was divided into many independent states, which until the seventeenth century were often at war with one another. This turbulent history meant that conditions were not always propitious for the cultivation of gardens. However, peace and prosperity did visit the different regions of Italy at different times, and were reflected in the creation of new gardens and the extension of old ones.

The Italian climate and landscape vary enormously from one end of the country to the other. In the north, with its high rainfall and relatively level terrain, gardens were easy to create but also easy to alter as fashion succeeded fashion. In the south, water shortage, poverty and constant political turmoil have meant that few gardens of note survive.

Very few medieval gardens survive in Italy, however there is ample written evidence throughout Europe to tell us what they were like. Pleasure gardens were generally small enclosed areas laid down to grass, with a central pool. The surrounding wall might have been covered with climbers such as honeysuckle, or with grapevines.

These simple meads were very different from the splendid pleasure-gardens created in Sicily after the ninth-century Arab conquest. They were all destroyed during the Norman invasion of 1091, but were probably similar to the Moorish gardens still to be seen in Spain. The Arabs did, however, leave one major legacy, for it was they who first imported the ubiquitous orange and lemon trees. The Normans, in their turn, made gardens in the Moorish style, although few survive (Villa Rufolo in Ravello is a rare exception, see page 183).

The great gift that Italian gardens have given to the rest of Europe is their reinterpretation of the classical traditions of the ancient world. At the beginning of the fifteenth century there was a widespread rediscovery of the classical authors. Study of their works led to a philosophy that came to be known as 'humanism'. This proved to be the key that unlocked the energies of the Renaissance.

The turning point of these early years was the publication, in 1452, of an architectural treatise by the Florentine Leon Battista Alberti. As a humanist Alberti looked to the classical authors for inspiration – Pliny the Younger and Vitruvius were his principal sources. His reinterpretation of the classical traditions of the ancient world was to determine the form taken by the early Renaissance gardens of Tuscany. He was not concerned so much with the layout of the garden as with its situation. Hillside sites were to be preferred, on account of the sun and cool breezes. There should be a fine view over 'the city, the owner's land, the sea or a great plain and familiar hills and mountains'. In the foreground 'there should be the delicacy of gardens'. An early Tuscan garden, Palazzo Piccolomini, displays this to perfection (page 107).

These gardens of the early Renaissance were designed with the utmost simplicity. The space was often divided by hedges into a series of enclosures or 'garden rooms'. Flowers played very little part in the design, and the garden was usually planted with evergreens and scented herbs.

Alberti's influence extended beyond the boundaries of the republic. His treatise served to forge an enduring link between the gardens of the classical and modern worlds, which soon became valid for the whole of Europe.

In the early years of the sixteenth century leadership in garden design passed from Tuscany to Rome, and it was here, with the patronage of the great princes of the Church, that the classical Renaissance style developed. Formerly, the architectural potential of the hillside sites, as advocated by Alberti, had been largely ignored. The new Roman style was characterised by the deliberate exploitation of the natural landscape to architectural ends. Hillsides were cut to form terraces linked by impressive flights of steps, tunnels and galleries. Both Bramante at the Vatican (page 170) and Raphael at Villa Madama (page 156) relied on classical sources. They naturally chose to adopt the imperial Roman style for their papal patrons. The gardens they made for the display of power and wealth were quite different from the modest designs of the early Renaissance. So, too, was their use of statues as an essential element. (Alberti had unwillingly conceded their occasional use 'if not indecent').

The gardens of the Renaissance reflected a secure and ordered world picture. Towards the middle of the sixteenth century, however, a sense of insecurity began to pervade the arts. It is sometimes said that it was caused by the barbaric violence of the Sack of Rome in 1527, a thrust at the very heart of the civilised world. This development of the Renaissance style is now known as Mannerism. Two significant developments characterise it in garden design. First, gardens changed from havens of peace and repose to places of discovery and entertainment, filled with water-powered automata and *giochi d'acqua*, or 'water tricks'. The latter took the form of water jets concealed throughout the garden. Only the owner knew where to find the controls, and this allowed him to soak his unlucky guests to the skin at will. The second development was the appearance of the 'iconographic' garden. By using the ornamentation and layout of his garden to refer to the then widely known events of classical mythology, the owner could express his philosophical ideals, and, if he wished, flatter himself or his patron. The fullest expression of both these developments is to be seen at the Villa d'Este, Tivoli (page 145).

Until the beginning of the seventeenth century the natural landscape had no place within the boundaries of the garden. Even the 'wild' aspect of the *bosco* owed more to artistry than nature. However, the fluid forms that typify the baroque in art found their expression in garden design in a new relationship with the landscape. The boundaries between art and nature became less distinct. The garden might merge into the encroaching forest (Villa Aldobrandini, page 134), or it might be completely dominated by the surrounding landscape (Cetinale, page 84). The most distinctive baroque garden of all is Isola Bella (page 17), with an architectural style that is at the same time flamboyant and in perfect harmony with its surroundings.

By the middle of the eighteenth century Italian garden design had lost much of its vitality. The formal French style had been adopted in many gardens in northern Italy. At the beginning of the nineteenth century the fashion for the English landscape garden spread across Italy, supplanting countless formal gardens whose unrecorded beauty is lost to us for ever.

ARTISTS AND WRITERS

Contemporary prints, engravings and descriptions are a valuable source of information about the original design of a garden and its subsequent history. Certain names will be found to recur frequently in the text. We have chosen to avoid repetition by giving information on them in this introduction.

G. B. Falda made engravings of the the great villas and monuments of Rome during the seventeenth century. **G. Zocchi** performed much the same task in Tuscany during the eighteenth century. **J. C. Volkamer**, an Austrian, published engravings of all the great gardens of the Veneto, and of specimens of the citrus fruit cultivated there. **Marcantonio dal Re**'s book of prints and descriptions of the villas in Lombardy was also published during the eighteenth century.

Another valuable source of information is to be found in the diaries of contemporary travellers. We have referred frequently to those of **John Evelyn**, the seventeenth-century English diarist who spent much time travelling in Italy. We have also drawn on the letters of **Président de Brosses**, a magistrate from Dijon, who travelled the length and breadth of the country during the eighteenth century.

At the beginning of this century the gardens of Italy were 'rediscovered' by foreign visitors. One of the most perceptive was the American author **Edith Wharton**. Her subtle and detailed analyses of individual gardens are as valid today as they were when her book *Italian Villas and their Gardens* was published in 1904. We have also included some magnificent garden plans by the English architect and garden designer **Harry Inigo Triggs**, first published in 1906. Among many subsequent publications, **Georgina Masson**'s beautifully photographed *Italian Gardens*, published in 1961, must still be regarded as the definitive book on the subject.

In recent years there has been a renewed interest in gardens among the Italians themselves. The FAI (La Federazione Ambientale Italiana) was set up with the aim of fulfilling much the same role as the National Trust in Britain. It has attracted a wide membership, and has also begun to assist in the management of certain gardens. Fortunately, many private owners and public administrators recognise the unique value and vulnerability of the gardens in their care, and they are both willing and able to meet the ever-increasing costs of maintaining them.

Our researches have taken us to the sites of several famous gardens that have been completely destroyed by urban development, neglect and vandalism. Despite their historic importance, they hardly merit a visit by even the most dedicated enthusiast. A poignant example is Andrea Doria's garden, which once covered the hillside above the Bay of Genoa. It has been replaced by an open-air cinema and a motorway flyover. Another is Villa Venaria Reale, which was originally the most spectacular of Turin's seventeenth-century gardens. It is now completely derelict. The famous garden of Pratolino (Parco Demidoff) near Florence met with a different form of destruction. The Austrian Duke Ferdinand objected to the cost of its upkeep, and had it replaced by an English landscape garden in 1819. Fortunately things have changed, and it is good to know that national concern for garden conservation is greater now than at any time this century. We hope that this book will encourage visitors to go to the gardens of Italy in increasing numbers, and swell the growing tide in favour of conservation and restoration.

PRACTICAL POINTS

In general, the optimum seasons for garden visiting run from mid-April to mid-June, and from the beginning of September to mid-October.

Some garden owners prefer visitors to make a prior appointment. This may nearly always be done by telephone, and we suggest that you approach the local tourist office (*azienda di soggiorno*) or your hotel for help.

Good maps are essential. We recommend the TCI (Touring Club Italiano) 1:200,000 series, in the green covers. These are widely available in Italy and are not expensive.

Many of the gardens in the book are privately owned, and you should not expect refreshments or lavatories to be provided. The text clearly indicates where these facilities are available.

Many of these gardens are built on steep slopes, and provision is rarely made for wheelchairs. The text indicates those gardens that are better suited to the wheelchair-bound visitor.

PIEDMONT (PIEMONTE)

Piedmont is the northernmost region of Italy, running from the Alps to the flat plains around the Po. The winters can be severe, although Lake Maggiore has its own mild microclimate.

The region has had a close relationship with France since the eleventh century, when the ruling house of Savoy gained possession of Turin. This is reflected in the design of some of its most important gardens. When, in 1697, Vittorio Amadeo II wanted to create a new garden for the ducal palace, he turned to Le Nôtre for help. Similarly, in 1740 Carlo Emanuele called in the French gardener Bernard to lay out the garden of his new 'hunting box' – actually the magnificent palace of Stupinigi.

Even Italian garden architects working in Piedmont had a tendency to adopt the details of French design. Green wooden boxes were used in place of terracotta pots for growing lemon trees, and the deciduous trees that grow so well in the region were planted in avenues in the French manner.

Sadly, we are unable to include Stupinigi in this edition, as it was closed for restoration at the time of writing. We have also omitted the gardens of Villa Regina and Venaria Reale, which were once so well known for their scale and beauty. They have been allowed to decay to such an extent that we feel they no longer merit inclusion in a guide book, although it is still possible to visit them.

Castello d'Agliè: the upper terrace.

CASTELLO D'AGLIÈ

SEVENTEENTH-CENTURY PALACE IN RURAL SETTING
• SEVENTEENTH- AND EIGHTEENTH-CENTURY GARDEN

HISTORY

The Castello d'Agliè was built for the family of San Martino d'Agliè in the early seventeenth century. The names of the architect and the garden designer are not recorded. The palace and its grounds are depicted in the 1682 collection of the possessions of the House of Savoy, known as the *Theatrum Sabaudiae*. Unfortunately, the accuracy of these prints can never be relied on. It was not mere artistic licence that led the artists to exaggerate the size and splendour of the buildings and gardens that were their subjects. Their imaginations were fired by the need to produce images that would glorify the Duchy of Savoy. However, Agliè is immediately recognisable. The vast mass of the building rises up from a terrace decorated with pots of lemon trees. The accuracy of many aspects of this print can be confirmed by the layout of the gardens today. At this time it was the home of Filippo d'Agliè, gentleman in waiting to the Duke of Savoy,, Master of the Armoury, Minister of Finance, poet, writer and a great favourite at court.

In 1764 Agliè was bought by Carlo Emanuele II for his son Benedetto Maurizio, Duke of Chablis. Alterations were made to the palace and the garden. During the Napoleonic occupation the park was separated from the rest of the property and bought by a lawyer called Genta. In the nineteenth century it returned to the House of Savoy, and was finally bought by the State in 1939.

THE GARDEN

The magnificent façade of the palace overlooks a wide terrace lined with lemon trees in faded green boxes. The arcaded entrance, which is linked to the *piano nobile* by a grand staircase, creates a shady extension to the terrace.

Below the terrace is the 'English' garden, which is reached by means of a double set of balustraded steps. It consists of a circular pool surrounded by a lawn and bounded by trees on two sides. According to the illustration in the *Theatrum Sabaudiae*, this pool already existed in the seventeenth cen-

tury. Then, instead of a single jet of water at its centre, it had an ornate baroque fountain. Pots of lemon trees decorated the area around the pool. The spaces on each side, which are now planted with trees, were then laid out as elaborate *parterres de broderie*. The whole of the eastern boundary, now obscured by trees, is shown as an arcaded retaining wall decorated with gushing fountains. This may be a fanciful elaboration, but if it ever existed it must have been a glorious sight.

The parterre garden, set between the retaining walls of the hanging garden and the upper terrace,

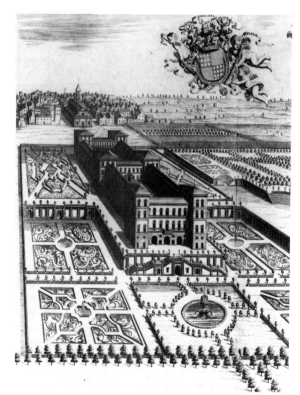

Above: *Castello d'Agliè.*
From the Theatrum
Sabaudiae, *1682.*
(Bodleian, 20503 a.4.)

Right: *Castello d'Agliè: an orange tree in a 'Versailles' box.*

is best seen from above. In the seventeenth-century print, the area is depicted as a *broderie* garden. The layout remains the same, with beds set out around a simple central pool. A deep nymphaeum is set into the retaining wall of the hanging garden. Telamones, or male caryatids, stand to either side of the arch and the keystone is decorated with a grotesque mask. Inside, despite these ferocious guardians, there is nothing but an eighteenth-century urn. The *Theatrum Sabaudiae* shows telamones flanking the shallower niches at each end of the wall, but if these ever existed they are no

longer there to be admired by the visitor.

Below the parterre garden there is an area of walled *bosco* which can be reached by steps concealed behind the box hedge. It was once set out as a series of winding walks lined with box hedges, which led to a central knoll. The knoll is still there, and so are the paths, but the whole is overgrown and neglected.

Returning to the upper terrace one proceeds along the west wall of the palace to the hanging garden. The whole of this side of the palace is given up to a long *limonaia* and a series of frescoed

Castello d'Agliè: the nymphaeum.

sculptures, executed by Ignazio and Filippo Collino in 1770, are said to represent the three tributaries of the River Po.

The fountain and the lawn in front of it form a huge semicircle. They are enclosed by the retaining wall of the curving ramps that lead to the balustraded terrace above. This wall was once decorated with stuccoed panels. Traces of soft yellow plaster mingle with the grey stone that has now been exposed beneath, forming a remarkably beautiful frame for the fountain. Each ramp is planted with an avenue, creating a boundary between the fountain and the wooded parkland to either side.

The park, which forms a perfect rectangle, stretches out above and beyond the fountain. It was laid out in its present style during the second half of the eighteenth century. Paths wind through the woods in the 'English manner' that was beginning to be fashionable at the time. There is a small lake at the far end of the park, with two islands, on which stand rustic summer houses.

garden rooms cooled by alabaster fountains. At the time of writing all of them were closed to the public while they awaited restoration. This is a sad loss to the visitor. Their beauty is enhanced by their air of gentle dereliction and the ivy that swamps the inner wall of the *limonaia*.

The hanging garden, which opens out at the end of the terrace, represents an impressive feat of seventeenth-century engineering. Unfortunately, it was also closed to the public at the time of writing, and was in a rather dishevelled state. The geometric layout depicted in the print of 1682 has been softened by the trees that are now dotted about the garden. The view, which must once have been pleasantly open, has been spoilt by modern buildings.

The park can be reached by following the terrace along the east wall of the palace. By turning right under the bridge below, one can walk directly to the fountain.

The *Theatrum Sabaudiae* shows an amphitheatre on the site now occupied by the fountain. The semicircular shape of the retaining wall behind the pool suggests that this may well have existed, and been used as a basis for the new construction. The

Castello d'Agliè	
Nearest major town:	Turin
Advance booking:	No
Owner:	The State
Address:	Agliè
Location:	Follow signs for the A5 to Aosta from the centre of Turin. Agliè is 33 km north of the city.
Open:	Summer: Thurs, Sat, Sun, 9–12, 1–7; Oct/Nov Sun only, 9–12, 1–6 . Hours subject to alteration.
Admission:	L2000, garden and palace
Wheelchairs:	No
Refreshments:	No
Lavatories:	Yes

ISOLA BELLA

SEVENTEENTH-CENTURY ISLAND GARDEN • WATER THEATRE

HISTORY

Isola Bella is one of the three Borromean islands which lie off Stresa on the western shore of Lake Maggiore. The Borromeo were a Milanese family of immense wealth, derived from their banking operations. Their most famous member is probably St Carlo Borromeo, whose determined attempts to reform the Church led directly to the Counter-Reformation. It was his nephew, Count Carlo III, who, in 1632, erected the first building on the island, a simple casino. Grander plans soon followed, and the island was slowly transformed by Carlo and his son Count Vitaliano IV.

The Borromeo employed Angelo Crivelli to draw up the original plans. After his death the work was continued by Carlo Fontana and Francesco Castelli, among many others. The 40 or so years the garden took to make are easily explained when one considers the task involved – transforming a barren, jagged rock into a base suitable for level terraces up to 100 ft high. Gilbert Burnet, the diarist and bishop, visited the island in 1685. In his words,

> . . . because the figure of the island was not made regular by Nature, they have built great Vaults and Portica's along the rock, which are all made grotesque, and so they have made it into a regular form by laying earth over these vaults.

Even before their completion the gardens had become famous throughout Europe, and were an obligatory halt on the Grand Tour. Countless famous figures have stayed here, among them Napoleon and Josephine after the Battle of Marengo had given them possession of Italy.

Curiously, Vitaliano halted construction of the palazzo in 1671, and it was not resumed until the 1950s. It is now being completed by Prince Borromeo-Arese, according to the original plans – surely one of the longer building projects in history.

Carlo Borromeo was devoted to his wife Isabella, and originally named the island after her. On his death, in 1652, she retired to a convent in nearby Arona. It was not long before the name was shortened to its present appropriate form. Let Bishop Burnet have the last word: 'the fragrant smell, the beautiful Prospect, and the delighting Variety that is here makes such a habitation for Summer that perhaps the whole world has nothing like it'.

Isola Bella. The Art of Garden Design in Italy, *Triggs, 1906. (Bodleian, 19187 b.6.)*

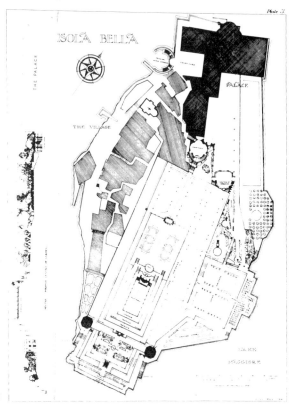

THE GARDEN

There is a unique sense of excitement in everything to do with this garden, right from the moment of leaving the faded art-nouveau boat station at Baveno. Isola Bella floats among the reflected mountains like the galley it was designed to resemble. Only the ram, at the northern (palazzo) end is missing, and it is likely that even this will one day be constructed.

The garden is now entered from the palazzo, which provides the opportunity to look at a useful model of the whole island in one of the reception rooms. The entrance lies through a most enchanting series of grottoes that lie beneath the palazzo. They are ornamented with shells and pebbles, and contain rare specimens of coral. The submarine colours used for decoration make this a wonderfully refreshing place on the hottest of days.

Nature's failure to make a regular 'figure' of the island meant that the garden was built markedly off-centre to the palazzo, although on entering the garden through the small Courtyard of Diana one is unlikely to be aware of the change of direction. To the left of the courtyard is the Theatre of Hercules. A central niche in the semicircular wall contains Hercules himself, with club and lionskin, while smaller niches on either side contain lesser divinities.

Having returned to the Courtyard of Diana, you make your way up the steps to a broad terrace, around which stroll the white peacocks claimed to be peculiar to these islands. At the far end rises

Isola Bella: putti above the water theatre.

Isola Bella's most astonishing *coup de théâtre*. This is the 'water theatre', an enchantingly delicate piece of baroque fantasy. Between the twin flights of stairs to the topmost terrace lies a semicircular wall with niches containing gods, goddesses and enormous scallops from which fountains play. Among the figures are Mars and Vulcan and representations of Agriculture and the Arts. From it ascend columns surmounted by putti, each in a different pose, and the whole is topped by the rampant figure of the Borromeo unicorn. The two reclining figures on either side are Toce and Ticino, the two principal rivers that feed Lake Maggiore.

Concealed above and behind the theatre is a broad stone terrace, which covers the huge garden reservoir. This terrace is the poop of the 'galley', complete even to the figurehead. This bears the Borromeo crown and their motto *'humilitas'* – rather less than apt in these gorgeous surroundings. From here one may look down over the 'stern' and count the ten terraces descending to the water's edge. Below, two hexagonal towers stand on either side, one a summerhouse and the other containing the pumps for the reservoir.

If you make your way down the steps on the eastern side you will arrive at the lower parterre garden on the fifth terrace. There is an aviary on one side of this, while the other overlooks the orange garden. The espaliered fruit trees have to be protected by temporary roofs during the winter.

Continuing round, you reach the southern tip of the island, laid out with *parterres de broderie*. The western side is the most recently planted (during the last century) and contains a number of exotic trees and shrubs, including magnificent camellias and magnolias. The planting elsewhere in the garden is much as it always was, although the trees have now grown so large that they blur the starkly dramatic lines of the original plan. Bishop Burnet refers to the walls as 'close covered with Oranges and Citrons'. De Brosses, in 1739, described the terraces as having trellises of jasmine, pomegranates or oranges, and the balustrades as being edged with pots of flowers. The mild climate means that garden designers have always used colour here with a freedom not found in the rest of Italy.

The exit is from the western side on the fifth terrace, through the village which, until recently, was occupied solely by the retainers of the Borromeo family.

Isola Bella	
Nearest major town:	Milan
Advance booking:	No
Owner:	Prince Borromeo-Arese
Address:	Lago Maggiore
Location:	The islands lie on the western side of Lake Maggiore. Ferries run from Stresa, Baveno and Pallanza. The cost is L7000 return, valid for unlimited trips between all three islands throughout the day. Boats leave every half-hour.
Open:	27 Mar–24 Oct, 9–12, 1.30–5.30
Admission:	Adults L6000, children L3000
Wheelchairs:	No
Refreshments:	Yes
Lavatories:	Yes

PALAZZO REALE

SEVENTEENTH-CENTURY FRENCH GARDEN BY LE NÔTRE

HISTORY

The garden of Palazzo Reale was designed by Le Nôtre for Vittorio Amadeo II, Duke of Savoy, and laid out between 1697 and 1702.

The site for the new garden was generally acknowledged to be 'difficult'. It consisted of an irregular space between the royal palace and the city walls. The size of the site was effectively tripled when Carlo Emanuele I, Vittorio Amadeo's father, demolished the fortifications to the east of the palace and replaced them with new walls in a slightly different position. It was evidently his intention to replace the existing baroque garden, thought to have been designed by Carlo Morello, with a larger and more grandiose design. The preliminary work of levelling the site and filling in the holes left by the demolition of the original walls, began in 1675. However, Carlo Emanuele's death put an end to further progress. Vittorio Amadeo was subsequently involved in a disastrous war with the French, and no further thought was given to the new garden until after the Treaty of Ryswick in 1697.

Vittorio Amadeo approached Le Nôtre through the Piedmontese ambassador in Paris. Almost exactly twenty years earlier Le Nôtre had been to Rome. On his return to France he pronounced the Italians 'absolutely ignorant' of the art of making gardens. It was perhaps with a sense of satisfaction at the thought of making a 'real' garden in Italy that he presented his proposed plans to the ambassador. The plans were duly sent on to the duke, accompanied by a letter in which the ambassador told him of the curiosity that the project was arousing in the French court.

Le Nôtre, who was 85 years old in 1697, did not travel to Turin himself. Having gained the duke's approval of his plans for the site, he entrusted their implementation to his pupil, De Marne. In a letter to one of the duke's ministers, he described De Marne as 'un très abile et honneste homme fort sage', and, with touching concern, begged that he should be given every comfort during his stay in Turin.

De Marne arrived in Turin during October 1697. In December he returned to Paris to consult Le Nôtre. (A contemporary architect might be suspected of allowing the lure of Christmas at home to affect his plans!) He continued to travel between Paris and Turin during the next six months. There can be no doubt that De Marne was well able to implement Le Nôtre's plans. As a mark of respect for his teacher, however, he chose to refer any difficulties that arose on site directly to him.

The essential layout of the garden was completed within the year. No further record of De Marne's presence in Turin can be found after June 1698, when he ordered 130 octagonal stone bases for pots, 160 square ones, and a quantity of marble for fountains and benches.

After De Marne's departure, Enrico Duparc became director of the garden. He was an architect, and it is thought that he supervised the completion of Le Nôtre's plans, adding some finishing touches of his own.

Over the years the garden has been altered. The urns and statues that stand among the trees are an eighteenth-century addition. The eastern end of the long entrance avenue was destroyed during the nineteenth century, and in 1920 Le Nôtre's design was cut in half by a new road linking Piazza Castello to Corso San Maurizio and Corso Regina Margherita.

THE GARDEN

The basis of Le Nôtre's design was to create three different areas within the garden, each with its own vista. The first was to the north of the palace, immediately in front of the gateway that leads from the inner courtyard. Although the planting may have changed, the long beds of the rose garden are much as they were originally conceived. The area is no longer decorated with rows of pots between the beds, but lime and plane trees still bound the garden to the right, just as Le Nôtre intended.

The second area is laid out at right angles to the rose garden. The original design was for two extensive parterres laid out to the east of the palace, and linked to it by a short flight of balustraded steps. The parterres have been replaced by two lawns divided by a gravel walk. The circular pool that lies on the far side of the parterre garden is ornamented with a massive rococo fountain attributed to Simone Martinez, who was director of the House of Savoy's sculpture studio. The principal figures are vast tritons playing conch shells. Dolphins, flowers and nymphs create a tangle of activity at water level, quite out of keeping with the simplicity of the rest of the garden.

The last of Le Nôtre's three vistas was formed by six radiating avenues, one of them over ¼ mile long. When the garden was divided by the new road at the beginning of this century, part of it was simply absorbed into the city. However, what remains of the great avenues constitutes perhaps the most beautiful, and the most recognisably French aspect of the garden. The climate of northern Italy favours deciduous trees, and they are widely used in gardens here. However, it was not usual to plant them in avenues. The evergreen cypress was preferred for such 'architectural' features.

We visited the garden in hazy autumn sunlight and were delighted by its simple lines and the charming eighteenth-century statues standing in the dappled shade. It is a municipal garden, however, and can suffer from the lack of atmosphere that so readily afflicts gardens that have been for many years without an owner.

Palazzo Reale.

Palazzo Reale	
Nearest major town:	Turin
Advance booking:	No
Owner:	The State
Address:	Piazza Castello, Torino
Location:	The palazzo is easily found in the centre of Turin with the aid of a streetmap from any *giornalaio* (news kiosk). It is nearly always possible to park in the piazza in front of the palazzo.
Open:	All year, 9–6 Palazzo: Tue–Sun, 9–1.30
Admission:	Garden free, palazzo L3000
Wheelchairs:	Yes
Refreshments:	No
Lavatories:	Yes

Palazzo Reale.

VILLA SAN REMIGIO

NINETEENTH-CENTURY TERRACED GARDEN • SPECTACULAR VIEWS OVER LAKE MAGGIORE

HISTORY

Villa San Remigio is named after the little church that abuts the garden. Its history is entwined with the lives of two families who bought land on the Castagnola hill above Lake Maggiore. Peter Browne, a British diplomat of Irish origin, bought his plot of land in 1859. Shortly afterwards he built a sort of Swiss chalet there, to which he retired with his large family. The fields adjoining Browne's property were bought by a Neapolitan marquis called Federico della Valle di Casanova. It was not long before one of Browne's daughters fell in love with the marquis and married him. The marriage resulted in the birth of their son, Silvio. Browne's eldest son, Dionysius, was already married. Sophie Browne, his second child, was destined to carry the union between the Brownes and the Casanova into a second generation by marrying Silvio. The land belonging to the two families was finally merged, and Sophie and Silvio began what was to be their life's work.

In 1903 Peter Browne's Swiss chalet was demolished to make way for Sophie and Silvio's new villa, which a local firm was employed to build in the Renaissance manner. In 1905 they constructed the terrace behind the villa, which overlooks the lake.

Little is known of the massive task of terracing the hillside to north and south of the house. However, it is said that Sophie built a model of the terraces in front of the house out of wood and cloth. She adjusted the model until she was happy with its effect at all times of the day. She even studied the effect of moonlight on the model terraces before she would allow the real garden to be built.

By 1916 both villa and garden were complete. The garden, which was tended by 30 gardeners, was opened to the public during the week.

Sophie della Valle di Casanova died at the age of 100 in 1960. In 1977 San Remigio was bought by the State, and it is now used as governmental regional offices.

THE GARDEN

'We are Silvio and Sophie della Valle di Casanova. Childhood united us, and this garden was born of the dreams that we shared in our youth. We planned it as children, and as man and wife we have created it.' This is a translation of Silvio and Sophie's introduction to the garden, engraved on a plaque behind the villa. The fruit of their youthful dreams is a romantic mixture of styles that ranges from the sacred grove to the winding paths of the eighteenth-century 'English' park. Lake Maggiore provides a breathtakingly beautiful backdrop to their creation.

Although the planting of the garden is being well maintained by the five gardeners employed by the Regione, its structure has reached a critical point of decay and some areas have already had to be closed to the public. It is ironic that the crumbling steps and overgrown paths should seem to heighten the della Valle family's romantic intention.

Sophie's carefully planned 'Renaissance' terraces lie below the southern façade of the villa. There are six of them in all, and they are linked to the house by a double flight of balustraded steps. The first terrace is characterised by mock-Roman fountains set into niches in the sustaining wall. The niches are decorated with mosaic festoons and dolphins. A series of shell seats, supported by dolphin pedestals set along the edge of a green lawn carpet, create the impression of an outdoor drawing room. This is accentuated by a curious armchair made of clipped yew. Statues of the four seasons by the eighteenth-century Paduan sculptor Francesco Rizzi crown the other garden wall.

The next terrace acts as a ceiling for the glorious winter garden that lies beneath. A vaulted grotto has been dug out beneath the terrace, and sealed with a glass wall. A stream runs through it, creating a marvellously warm and steamy atmosphere which proved to be ideal for growing sub-tropical plants. The marquis took several romantic pictures of his wife amidst ferns and orchids, which may still be seen in the museum archives in Pallanza.

The Hour Garden, so named because of the circular stone sundial at its centre, occupies the same terrace as the winter garden. The sundial is decorated with the signs of the zodiac and an inscription which, roughly translated, reads:

Put here by Silvio and Sophie so that the new light of day may dispel the shadows of fled hours.

The statues that decorate the balustrade are by Orazio Miranali. They represent Juno, Bacchus, Venus and Pluto.

A second winter garden, twice the length of the first, stands above the lowest terrace. This terrace is known as the Garden of Happiness. It is occupied by a series of *parterres de broderie*, laid out around a central pool, and divided by pebble mosaic paths. A magnificent fountain by Riccardo Ripamonti stands in the pool. It is known as 'the Triumph of Diana'. The goddess stands in a shell chariot pulled by two web-footed horses.

Wrought-iron balconies overlook the lowest terrace, or Garden of Sadness, and the steps down to it are guarded by gryphons with iron wings. While the Garden of Happiness was originally

planted with innumerable roses, the Garden of Sadness has always been filled with mournful ever-greens. It is occupied by two pools set into lawns which are bounded by box and an elaborate wrought-iron fence. A nymphaeum, decorated with mosaics and the family crest, shelters a statue of Hercules killing the Hydra, by Giovanni Marchiori. Stone seats shaded by topiary columns are set against the retaining wall.

Next to the little church of San Remigio, reached by taking the path that leads down through the woods from the second terrace, there is an area which seems to be intended as a sacred grove. Cypresses shade a simple central pool, and a statue of Pan by Ripamonti stands guard.

The true scale of these gardens only becomes apparent when one realises that the entire hillside below the villa was cultivated as an 'English' garden which ran down to the lake. The winding paths, steps and terraces that led down through the trees are now largely overgrown. The woods are made up of a strange mixture of bog oak, cedar, chestnut, bamboo, Japanese privet, camphor and rhododendrons.

Above the 'English' garden there is a long arcaded gallery where ivy and wisteria run riot. Steps lead up through a tunnel to the terrace behind the villa.

The two 'seventeenth-century' terraces to the north of the villa are known as the Garden of Sighs and the Garden of Memories. Among the statues in the Garden of Sighs are the effigies of Sophie and Silvio.

Villa San Remigio: the Garden of Sadness.

Villa San Remigio	
Nearest major town:	Milan
Advance booking:	No
Owner:	Regione di Piemonte
Address:	Salita San Remigio, Pallanza
Location:	Pallanza is on the west side of Lake Maggiore on the ss34. Follow signs for Intra from the town centre. Turn left immediately after Piazza Giovanni XXIII, taking Via Cavallina. Villa signposted to left. (Sign obscured by creepers.)
Open:	Mon–Fri, 9–12.30
Admission:	Free
Wheelchairs:	No
Refreshments:	No
Lavatories:	No

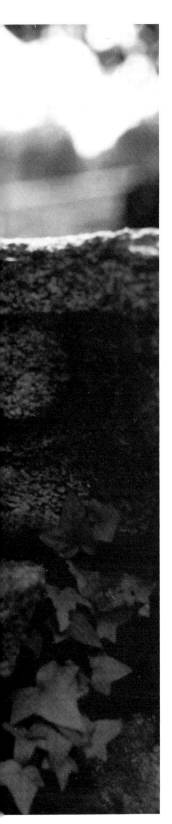

LOMBARDY (LOMBARDIA)

Lombardy lies in the north of the country. Its landscape comprises the Alps, the Italian lakes and the vast flat valley of the Po. The climate, like that of neighbouring Piedmont, can be harsh in winter, and has a high annual rainfall.

The region's varied geography has given rise to a range of gardens that cannot be classified under any one stylistic group. The impact of the Renaissance was keenly felt in the area, and towards the end of the sixteenth century gardens took on the elaborate architectural appearance that originated in Rome.

Edith Wharton was the first to identify the potential danger facing the gardens of those with too much, rather than too little money. The ease with which their owners could embrace changing fashions led to regular bouts of destruction and rebuilding. This was certainly the case in Lombardy, where many sixteenth-century gardens were destroyed during the eighteenth century to accommodate fashionable 'English' parks. In the Po Valley this operation was rendered all the easier by the flat terrain.

Villa d'Este: detail of the water staircase.

IL BOZZOLO

SEVENTEENTH-CENTURY TERRACED GARDEN • OAK AVENUE • FRESCOED APSE

HISTORY

Very little is known about the history of Il Bozzolo and its garden. The villa was built at the beginning of the sixteenth century for the della Porta family, and the garden was laid out during the first half of the seventeenth century. Its design is sometimes attributed to Gianangelo della Porta.

The property passed by marriage out of the della Porta and into the Ferrari family at the end of the eighteenth century. Since the nineteenth century it has been owned by the Bozzolo family.

The future of Il Bozzolo is, however, uncertain. At the time of writing it was about to be sold, and might either be bought by the FAI or by the Comune of Casalzuigno. If the FAI buys it, the garden is likely to be restored and opened to the public on a regular basis. If it is bought by the Comune the situation will probably remain much as it is today.

THE GARDEN

Il Bozzolo is set on the side of a steep wooded valley overlooking the Alps. It is an overwhelming landscape, and yet through its simple and perfectly balanced design the garden succeeds in framing and incorporating its surroundings without being dwarfed by them. In so doing it exemplifies that peculiarly Italian skill of creating an absolute bond

Villa il Bozzolo.

between the layout of a garden and the landscape that surrounds it.

A powerful horizontal perspective is formed by four stone terraces which run the width of the garden. These terraces, with their balustrades and the graceful flight of steps that links them, can be seen spreading out across the hillside from the road below. What cannot be appreciated from below is their surprising length and depth. Each terrace extends away from the steps beyond the line of vision, and has a breadth of about 30 ft. The terraces are rather like a series of enclosed gardens, filled with the sound of running water from the shell fountains that decorate the walls. On each retaining wall espaliered fruit trees flourish, while the balustrades are decorated with stone urns overflowing with fruit. At the end of each balustrade a putto stands guardian over the steps, each one striking a different pose.

The horizontal perspective created by the terrace seems to establish the garden's place in the landscape, while the avenue of cypresses, cutting through the woods on the hillside above, succeeds in drawing that landscape into the garden. The avenue is now largely overgrown, which is scarcely surprising when one considers that the whole property is maintained by a single gardener. However, the path of the avenue may still be traced and its effect is felt in the garden.

The villa is not incorporated into this powerfully linear design. It stands below the terraces, facing away from the central perspective and overlooking a small lawn that may once have been planted as parterres. Across the lawn a magnificent avenue of oaks leads away to a frescoed apse. The avenue is over 100 yards long, and the oak trees create a mottled shade quite unlke the zebra stripes of a cypress avenue. The apse, which is frescoed with gods and goddesses in a sylvan scene, provides a delightful setting for the occasional summer concert.

Between the terraces and the wooded hillside there is a sloping, semicircular meadow. This feature represents the most curious, and perhaps the most skilful aspect of the garden's design. It is divided from the surrounding countryside by a low stone wall and a bank. The addition of cypresses, planted to follow the line of the wall, strengthens the visual boundary between the garden and the hillside. By enclosing a portion of the surrounding country-

side, the architect hit on the simplest possible way of increasing the apparent size of the garden, thus bringing it into proportion with the landscape beyond.

The meadow is crowned by a double flight of balustraded steps leading to a small terrace. Signora Bozzolo told us that her children used to swim in the pool that lies immediately below the terrace – a perfect vantage point from which to look back at the garden and enjoy the grandeur of its setting.

Il Bozzolo	
Nearest major town:	Varese
Advance booking:	Yes
Owner:	Signora Bozzolo
Address:	Viale Sen. Prof. Camillo Bozzolo, Casalzuigno
Location:	Casalzuigno lies approx. 20 km north west of Varese. From Varese take ss394 for Laveno. After 17 km turn right to Brenta and Casalzuigno. The villa is signposted to the left on the far side of the village.
Open:	Villa currently open on certain Sundays in summer. Alternatively, appointments may be made through the Comune in Casalzuigno. Readers may prefer to do this with the help of the tourist office in Laveno or Varese.
Admission:	Free
Wheelchairs:	No
Refreshments:	No
Lavatories:	No

VILLA CARLOTTA

EIGHTEENTH-CENTURY FORMAL GARDEN • LAKESIDE SETTING • FINE BOTANICAL GARDENS

HISTORY

The construction of Villa Carlotta was begun in 1690 for Marshal Giorgio Clerici (architect unknown) and was completed by 1745. Fifty years later it passed by marriage into the hands of Giovanni Sommariva, who, among other alterations, added the unfortunate pediment and clock to the villa. In 1843 the property was given as a wedding present from Princess Marianna of Prussia to her daughter Charlotte, Duchess of Saxe-Meiningen, hence its present name. She and her husband were responsible for the creation of the large landscape garden with its wide range of species, made feasible by the mild local climate. On the outbreak of war in 1914, the villa was confis-

Villa Carlotta.

cated by the Italian Government and has remained State property. Since 1927 the house and grounds have been carefully maintained under the management of the Ente Villa Carlotta.

THE GARDEN

Before buying your entrance ticket, it is worth crossing the road (taking your life in your hands) to stand on the steps of the watergate. This is where you would originally have arrived to enjoy a fine view of the villa with its mountain background reflected in the lake. It is from here that the perfect symmetry of the double stairs leading to the villa is best appreciated. The fine wrought-iron gates in front of you, with their gilded Cs and columns surmounted by figures of the four seasons, are no longer opened. The present entrance lies to the left, by the neoclassical Sommariva family chapel.

Inside the original entrance lies a small central pool with a delightful fountain of a boy with a dolphin. This is surrounded by box hedges laid out in the form of coronets filled with begonias. On either side dense *boschi* hem in the visitor. These replace what was once a delicate *parterre de broderie* running the width of the garden.

Three narrow terraces lie between this area and the villa. The geometrical lines of the ascending balustrade are softened by the climbing roses, vines and trailing geraniums with which it is covered. Fern-filled wall fountains refresh the visitor climbing up to the villa, while a pergola on the second level leads past orange and lemon trees. In this temperate climate these have been planted directly into the ground rather than in pots.

Passing through the villa, with its collection of statues by sculptors such as Canova, you find a dark grotto set into the cliff behind the house. Looking back, the villa gives the impression of being filled with light.

Turning to the right here takes you into the heart of the landscape garden, which is maintained by a staff of ten. The outstanding collection of azaleas and rhododendrons are well worth visiting when they are at their peak from late April to June.

Villa Carlotta	
Nearest major town:	Como
Advance booking:	No
Owner:	The State
Address:	Tremezzo, Lago di Como Tel: 0344-40405/41011
Location:	Tremezzo lies 30 km north of Como on the western side of the lake. From Como take the ss340 for Menaggio and Gravedona. The villa is clearly signposted, and is situated on the lake between Tremezzo and Cadenabbia.
Open:	Daily from 1 Mar–31 Oct – Mar, Oct 9–11.30 and 2–4.30; Apr–Sep 9–6
Admission:	L4000
Wheelchairs:	Yes, with assistance
Refreshments:	No
Lavatories:	Yes

VILLA CICOGNA

SIXTEENTH-CENTURY GARDEN • SUNKEN GARDEN • WATER STAIRCASE

HISTORY

Villa Cicogna has been the home of the Cicogna family for over 400 years. It was originally built as a hunting lodge by the Mozzoni family in the fifteenth century. Over the years they came to use the lodge with increasing frequency, eventually expanding it, having it frescoed inside and out, and turning it into their main residence.

In 1592 Asciano Mozzoni died, leaving the villa to his daughter Angela. It was through her marriage to Gianpietro Cicogna that the property came into the Cicogna family. They transformed it into a magnificent Renaissance villa and laid out most of the existing garden. Sadly, there is no record of the name of the garden architect whom they employed.

The terrace garden to the north of the villa was a seventeenth-century addition, and in the eighteenth century the woods above the villa were transformed into an 'English' park. The property is now under the protection of the FAI, with whose help the garden is being carefully restored.

THE GARDEN

The gardens of Villa Cicogna are laid out on the side of a steep slope. The visitor enters through an arcaded courtyard at the lowest of the garden's three levels. The arcades, exquisitely frescoed with a trellis of leaves and flowers, putti and peacocks, herald one's first glimpse of the garden, bathed in sunlight beyond the shadowy courtyard. This garden is enclosed on one side by the courtyard and the villa, and on the other three sides by high

Villa Cicogna: the water staircase.

32

walls. On the right, the retaining wall of the upper terrace is decorated with niches containing busts and statues. The boundary wall, on the opposite side of the garden, is covered in ivy. It has a nymphaeum set into it which shelters a statue of Mercury. The far wall, which is of equal height, contains a grotto. At the time of writing this was being restored and contained nothing but a complex web of pipes for *giochi d'acqua*. The garden is laid out in a regular pattern of box hedges, lawns and colourful beds of begonias and geraniums. Below the retaining wall there are two rectangular balustraded fishponds of considerable size. The fountains at the centre of each pool fill the enclosed space with the sound of running water.

It is fitting that this sunken garden, with its atmosphere of peace and privacy, should be linked to the lower and less formal part of the villa. The reception rooms of the *piano nobile* open onto the wide upper terrace, which is so different in scale and purpose to the intimate garden below.

The terrace is linked to the sunken garden by a flight of steps which lead up through a tunnel to the left of the grotto. One enters the tunnel through a pair of wrought-iron gates decorated with a stork, the *cicogna* from the family coat of arms.

The balustraded terrace runs the width of the garden. At its southern end it provides a vantage point from which to enjoy the bright parterre beds and the shimmering pools below. It passes between the villa and the base of the water staircase, ending beyond the boundary of the seventeenth-century terrace garden to the north of the villa. The terrace represents that essential element of a Renaissance garden: a sheltered walk offering views over the garden and the surrounding countryside. On a clear day one can see Lake Lugano in the far distance. A raised rose walk runs parallel to the terrace, broken only at its mid-point by two supine maidens, who flank the base of the water staircase.

The staircase was designed to be seen from the windows of the *piano nobile*, and it is only from inside the villa that the intended perspective can be truly appreciated. Rising steeply from its base to a pavilion on the crest of the hill, it creates an effective visual link between the lower garden and the *bosco* above. This exploitation of the natural landscape to architectural ends betrays the influence which the great gardens of the Roman Renaissance were already exerting on the designers of the north.

The water that feeds the staircase originally came from a spring, and was carried through the woods in its own little aqueduct. It is now pumped up from below, but it is fun to trace the old route through the woods of the 'English' park.

At its northern end the terrace leads into a sloping grove of yew and beech. A path leads through the grove, past the remains of a balustraded terrace and fountain, and up to the pavilion at the head of the water staircase. Beyond the pavilion the *bosco* merges with the eighteenth-century park. Today red squirrels abound in these woods, where once the Mozzoni family and their guests hunted bears and wild boar.

Villa Cicogna	
Nearest major town:	Varese
Advance booking:	No
Owner:	Countess Cicogna Mozzoni
Address:	Villa Cicogna, Bisuschio, Varese
Location:	Bisuschio lies 8 km north of Varese on the ss344 for Porto Ceresio and Ponte Tresa. The villa is on the left just through Bisuschio. Parking is available on the right, opposite the entrance to the villa.
Open:	Apr–Oct, Sun only, 9–12, 3–7
Admission:	L3000 adult, L1800 child, villa and garden
Wheelchairs:	No
Refreshments:	No
Lavatories:	Yes

VILLA D'ESTE

FINE SIXTEENTH-CENTURY DOUBLE WATER STAIRCASE
● LAKESIDE SETTING ● HOTEL

HISTORY

Despite its name, the Villa d'Este has never been connected with the famous Este family of Ferrara. It was built in 1568 for Tolomeo Gallio, the son of a Como family, on his appointment as a cardinal. He commissioned the Lombard architect Pellegrino Tibaldi to build three villas on the lake, the others being at Lenno (Villa Balbianello) and Gravedona. Villa Garrovo, as the villa at Cernobbio was originally known, became Cardinal Gallio's principal residence. After the cardinal's death, however, it gradually fell into neglect, before eventually passing into the hands of the Jesuits.

At the end of the eighteenth century the villa was acquired by Marquis Bartolomeo Calderara for his wife Vittoria Peluso, a famous dancer known as 'La Pelusiña'. She restored the villa and began the alteration of the gardens. She was responsible for the extraordinary mock fortifications, built to flatter her second husband, Dominique Pirro, who had been one of Napoleon's generals.

Villa d'Este. The Art of Garden Design in Italy, *Triggs, 1906. (Bodleian, 19187 b.6.)*

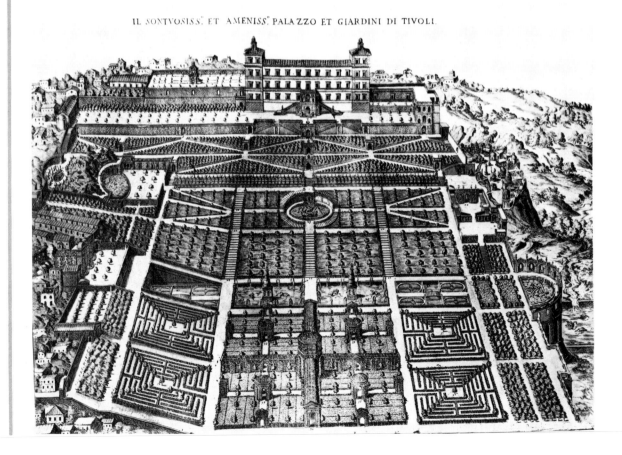

IL SONTVOSISS.º ET AMENISS.º PALAZZO ET GIARDINI DI TIVOLI.

In 1815 Villa Garrovo was bought by Princess Caroline of Brunswick, the dissolute, eccentric and neglected wife of the British Prince Regent. In a fanciful moment she changed its name to Villa d'Este, and restyled both villa and garden in the fashion of the time. After her death, the villa changed hands several times. In 1856 it was first opened as a hotel by Baron Ciani. Following a short ownership by the Empress Maria Fedorowna of Russia, it was re-opened in 1873, and is now among Europe's most famous hotels.

THE GARDEN

In the course of its many changes of function and ownership, nearly all of Tibaldi's garden has been lost. However, we are lucky that the superb double water staircase is among the few surviving original features. Unusually for a garden of such pronounced Roman influence, this is off-centre in relation to the villa, but Tibaldi undoubtedly intended that the outstanding view of the lake should not be obstructed. As a result, the visitor approaching by water would have been able to gaze straight up the long avenue of cypress and magnolia trees to the nymphaeum at the summit. It is well worth enjoying this wonderful perspective by doing as we did, and having tea seated by the lake. While doing this, remember that the space in front of you (now lawn) was originally, and until quite recently, occupied by four large parterres. (Perhaps the management might consider reinstating these?)

Beyond this space, and framing the water staircase, is a series of splendidly theatrical 'wings', decorated in shell and pebble mosaic and topped with obelisks. These were once intended to be roofed-in to form garden pavilions linking the villa to the present *limonaia*, but were never completed.

Steps lead up around a central fishpond to the foot of the water staircase. This crosses the lakeside road by means of a bridge. It is unusual in being a double stair, so that the visitor has the charming experience of climbing the broad *tapis vert*, striped with sunlight and shadow, with the sight and sound of falling water on either side. At the top stands an elaborately decorated and bat-filled nymphaeum. This contains a dramatic statue of the dying Hercules, maddened with pain, hurling his companion, Lichas, into the water.

On either side of the avenue the grounds have been terraced, and were originally probably simply planted with olives or vines. A bridge leads across the Garrovo stream to the maze of paths with which the cliffs are covered. These lead to the forts, battlements, pavilions and waterfalls which exemplify the fevered excesses of the Romantic imagination.

Villa d'Este	
Nearest major town:	Como
Advance booking:	Yes, unless using hotel facilities.
Owner:	Villa d'Este
Address:	Cernobbio, Lago di Como
Location:	Cernobbio lies 5 km north of Como on the western side of the lake. From Como take ss340 for Menaggio and Gravedona. The villa is clearly sign-posted in Cernobbio.
Open:	1 Apr–31 Oct. Open to hotel guests, or by appointment with Giovanna Salvadore (public relations) Tel: 031-511471/512471
Admission:	Free
Wheelchairs:	Yes
Refreshments:	Yes
Lavatories:	Yes

Villa Negrotto.

LIGURIA

The region of Liguria lies between Piedmont and the sea. Sheltered by mountains from the cold northerly winds, and facing south over the Mediterranean, its climate is mild throughout the year.

Genoa, the capital, has varied in importance over the centuries. In the fourteenth century it was defeated by Venice in the struggle for maritime power. The city enjoyed a burst of confidence and a brief period of independence during the sixteenth century under the leadership of Admiral Andrea Doria.

The ideal climate along this coast has always inspired the creation of gardens in a wide range of styles. Sadly, few gardens now remain. Genoa, once famous as a city of gardens stretching from the sea to the hills above, lost almost all of them to nineteenth-century urban development. Andrea Doria's Palazzo Doria, often described by travellers as being among the finest Renaissance gardens in Italy, survived into the present century. The upper garden was destroyed within months of Edith Wharton's visit in 1903. The lower garden survived until quite recently when, with an insensitivity to their heritage that defies belief, the Genoese built a motorway flyover across it, and turned what remained into an open-air cinema.

VILLA DURAZZO PALLAVICINI

NEOCLASSICAL GARDEN • LAKE • TEMPLES

HISTORY

By the early years of the nineteenth century the Italian Riviera had already become a magnet for the foreign visitor, not least because of the mildness of its climate and, consequently, its spectacular exotic gardens. It was with this in mind that Marquis Ignazio Pallavicini decided to create a romantic park near his villa at Pegli in 1837. He employed the painter Michele Carizio to draw up the designs. On completion it was opened to the public and was instantly successful, both with the local population and with an increasing number of foreign visitors. It has remained open for the last 150 years and, despite the attentions of graffiti-barbarians, retains all its slightly vulgar charm.

. . . a brummagem creation . . . to which the guidebooks still send throngs of unsuspecting tourists, who come back imagining that this tawdry jumble of weeping willows and Chinese pagodas, mock Gothic ruins and exotic vegetation, represents the typical 'Italian garden' . . .

Villa Durazzo Pallavicini.

Edith Wharton's words, written at the turn of the century, do less than justice to a garden that has given pleasure for so long to so many. It is important to remember that Carizio's secondary occupation was as a theatrical set designer, and one should perhaps regard the garden as an absurd and two-dimensional joke.

THE GARDEN

A very long avenue winds up to the villa between ilex and palm trees, crossing the railway en route. It opens eventually onto the terrace in front of the villa. The view over the Bay of Genoa must once have been superb, but one now looks out over the shoddy post-war building that has infested every inch of ground between the villa and the sea. Below lies the botanical garden of one Clelia Grimaldi. A statue commemorates her botanical knowledge.

The current way of entering the garden seems unnecessarily complex: along a fire-escape attached to the cliff face below the villa, past palms and camphor trees, up a steep flight of steps past the neo-Gothic chapel and finally into a long avenue leading to the entrance of the garden proper. This is a neoclassical arch with a pavilion above it. A Latin inscription advises the visitor as follows: 'Farewell to those urban cares that trouble the soul; I am called by the high mountains, woods, fountains and all that is sublime and eloquent in Nature and raises the spirit to God'.

A box walk beyond this leads past a simple fountain under the overhanging trees to a matching arch at the far end. As you pass through this it suddenly transforms itself into a rustic hut. This apparently whimsical juxtaposition perhaps offers a clue to the designer's intention. Here you are in no place and no period, but at any moment may find yourself in another continent, another century – here you cannot help but leave your 'urban cares' behind.

Steep paths past grottoes and cascades lead up through the *bosco* to the lake. A boat lies rotting in the undergrowth, evoking scenes of holidays long ago when boating parties would explore the lakeside grottoes, and be drenched by the *giochi d'acqua* with which they were fitted. Their friends would enjoy the spectacle through holes pierced in the grotto ceilings, before losing themselves in the maze. Children might swing out over the water on the iron swing that still stands by the water's edge. Lovers, doubtless, would be found everywhere, from the Mogul pavilion to the summerhouse with its mirror-covered walls and *broderie* garden dedicated to Flora.

The boats no longer cross the lake, but otherwise little has changed. Today families stand on the wrought-iron bridge to feed the turtles and the enormous carp, a picnic is taking place beneath the weeping willow, and a pair of oblivious lovers occupy the Chinese pagoda. Proof, as if it were needed, of how little human pleasures change.

Villa Durazzo Pallavicini	
Nearest major town:	Genoa
Advance booking:	No
Owner:	Comune di Genova
Address:	Via Martiri della Libertà, Pegli, Genova
Location:	Pegli lies about 10 km west from the centre of Genoa in the direction of Savona. The villa entrance is close to the station and next to the PCI (Communist Party) club.
Open:	All year from 8.00. Closing times as follows: Jan 5.30 May–Aug 7.30 Feb 6.00 Sep 6.30 Mar 6.30 Oct 5.30 Apr 7.00 Nov–Dec 5.00
Admission:	Free
Wheelchairs:	No
Refreshments:	No
Lavatories:	No

LA MORTOLA

LARGE BOTANICAL GARDEN OVERLOOKING THE SEA

HISTORY

Sir Thomas Hanbury, an English businessman with a passionate interest in horticulture, bought La Mortola in May 1867. The property comprised 112 acres of rough ground and olive groves dropping 300 feet to the sea.

Sir Thomas and his brother Daniel, a pharmacologist with a particular interest in medicinal plants, wanted to create a botanical garden where exotic plants could be acclimatised and then allowed to live naturally among indigenous species. A combination of climatic and geographical conditions created an ideal environment at La Mortola for this venture. The only problems were the long dry summers and the poor and rocky soil. With the help of local labour these problems were overcome. Several underground reservoirs and irrigation channels were built, and the soil received intensive preparation. Even after this initial period the Hanburys continued to employ most of the adult population of the village in the house or the garden. Sir Thomas became an influential local figure; he built the local school at Latte and the flower market in Ventimiglia.

In December 1868 Sir Thomas hired a professional gardener called Ludwig Winter. He worked at La Mortola for six years, and in that time he imposed on the garden the structure that it retains to this day. The steep terraces were stocked with plants from nurseries throughout Europe. As the garden gained a reputation, donations began to arrive, and Sir Thomas soon built up a collection of plants, from temperate regions all over the world, which covered an area of 49 acres. At the end of the century the director of Kew Gardens declared that La Mortola had 'no rival among the principal collections of living plants in the world'.

It is scarcely surprising that the gardens soon began to attract illustrious visitors. Queen Victoria, whose disapproval of gambling led her to spurn the hospitality of Monte Carlo, stayed with the Hanburys in 1882. Over the years other guests ranged from Mussolini to Kuo Sung Tao, the first Chinese diplomat to be sent to Britain and France.

To commemorate his visit he wrote the Chinese character 'fo', meaning happiness, on the arch at the entrance to the garden.

Sadly, Daniel Hanbury died in 1875. However, Sir Thomas had 32 more years to work at extending and developing the garden before his death in 1907.

In 1912 the third edition of the *Hortus Mortolensis* was printed. This was a catalogue of all the species in the garden, and on this occasion it contained 5,300 entries.

Cecil Hanbury and his wife Dorothy inherited the garden in 1920. Their interests were more aesthetic than botanical, and under their care various alterations were made to the planting and layout.

During the Second World War La Mortola became a minefield, and both the villa and the garden were badly damaged. In the post-war years the whole question of restoring and maintaining the property became in insoluble problem. In 1960 Lady Dorothy handed it over to the State, thus initiating a long and complex period in its history that has almost proved to be fatal. Responsibility for the garden has passed among three principal bodies: the University of Genoa, the Sovraintendenza per i Beni Ambientali e Architettonici di Liguria, and the Istituto Internazionale di Studi Liguri. Between 1980 and 1987 it had no owner at all. The gardeners were unpaid, and those who left were not replaced. Many of the plants which survived the ensuing neglect were killed by the severe frosts of 1985 and 1986, leaving less than 1,500 species. The steps and terraces have been allowed to decay to such an extent that only a third of the garden area can now be opened to the public, and only eight gardeners are employed to maintain it. Very little remains in the way of usable greenhouses and propagation facilities.

A new wave of concern about the plight of the garden has resulted in the foundation of The Friends of the Hanbury Botanic Garden. The organisation has an international membership united by the aim of returning the garden to its former splendour. (For details write c/o The Royal Horticultural Society, PO Box 313, Vincent Square, London SW10 2PE.)

THE GARDEN

The Victorian gateway built by Sir Thomas Hanbury is still the main entrance to La Mortola. It frames a breathtaking view of the garden, with the sea creating a serene backdrop against which a mass of flowers and foliage fall steeply away at your feet. Descending the labyrinth of winding paths through waves of scent and colour, it is hard to believe that little more than a hundred years ago this was simply a barren hillside. La Mortola is still a remarkable collection, despite the evidence of neglect and frost damage that is to be seen in almost every area of the garden. Even if this were not true, the garden would still be worth visiting for the beauty of the site alone.

Immediately below the entrance is the small villa where Lady Dorothy passed the last years of her life. The house is still owned by the family. Almost at once the path divides, and one is faced with the first of the numerous choices that have to be made in the course of the long descent. Each path leads between beds where plants from the Cape of Good Hope, Mexico, Ethiopia and Australia, to name but a few of the countries of origin, are mixed with indigenous species just as the Hanbury brothers intended. The skyline is punctuated by a curious mixture of trees. Native olives and cypresses are interspersed with palms, pittosporum, eucalyptus, exotic oaks and Aleppo pines.

Sir Thomas's interests were not restricted to horticulture. He was a great collector, with a particular interest in classical antiquity. When restoration work on the villa is complete, it is to be used to house the Hanbury collection. While the work is in progress the building is rather a bleak sight. However, there is still a magnificent view, over the lower garden to the sea, from the terrace that Sir Thomas added to the south side of the villa.

The area in front of the villa was laid out as a parterre garden. Box and lavender hedges surrounded beds of medicinal herbs planted by Daniel Hanbury. A few overgrown lavender bushes are all that remain of the layout.

It is in the area immediately surrounding the villa that Lady Dorothy's touch can most clearly be seen. Here are the remains of a pergola, intended

to be the longest in Europe, and a small enclosed garden with brick paths, which has a remarkably English feel to it. Hanbury's son and daughter-in-law also had flights of elegant, semicircular steps built between the terraces all over the garden, although many are now too dilapidated to be used.

A cypress avenue leads down from the mausoleum of Sir Thomas and his wife towards the sea. Beyond the avenue the path is crossed by the Via Giulia Augusta, the ancient Roman road that cuts through the garden. The road runs along a deep trench, an interesting demonstration of the extent to which the soil level has risen over the last 2,000 years.

The citrus grove beyond the road represents a fascinating collection which includes a specimen of the Shadock grapefruit, bearing fruit weighing over 3 lbs.

An attractive bar and restaurant have recently been built at the lowest level of the garden.

La Mortola	
Nearest major town:	Ventimiglia
Advance booking:	No
Owner:	University of Genoa
Address:	Capo Mortola, Ventimiglia
Location:	Clearly signposted from the Ventimiglia exit off the autostrada.
Open:	Summer 9–6 Winter 10–4
Admission:	L8500 adult, L4500 child
Wheelchairs:	No
Refreshments:	Yes
Lavatories:	Yes

VILLA NEGROTTO

NINETEENTH-CENTURY GARDEN • GOTHIC REVIVAL VILLA

HISTORY

The Villa Negrotto has a considerably longer history than one might imagine from its present appearance. In its original form it was a simple watchtower, known to have been standing in 1255. In 1558 the land was bought by Tobia Pallavicino, who enlarged the tower into a castle. In 1825 Alessandro Pallavicino employed Ippolito Cremona, a Swiss engineer, to lay out the gardens, which included 6 miles of carriage driveway. Alessandro's grand-daughter married Lazzaro Negrotto Cambiaso, who, in 1880, had the castle entirely reconstructed in the Gothic Revival manner by the architect Rovelli. The original watchtower was rebuilt with a huge new loggia.

The fine 'Liberty'-style greenhouse was built by Lamberto Cusani for the Marchesa Matilda Negrotto-Cambiaso Giustiniani. The estate was opened to the public for the first time in 1986, when it passed into the ownership of the Comune di Arenzano, whose offices it now houses.

Villa Negrotto.

THE GARDEN

This garden provides an interesting contrast to the neoclassical garden of Villa Durazzo, laid out only a few years later. It cannot be considered as representative of any particular period, but simply as containing all the features that brought pleasure to the hearts of Alessandro Pallavicino and his successors.

The entrance avenue of ilex soon gives way to well-grown stands of the palm trees that also appear in every corner of the grounds. On the left lies open parkland, while on the right a stream descends through the woods via pools and cascades. At the head of the avenue, in front of the villa, is a pool decorated with the traditional Ligurian mosaic and occupied by turtles (further proof of the mildness of the climate).

Immediately behind the villa lies the upper terrace, which is linked to the *piano nobile* by a bridge. Two large grottoes lie beneath this. (The spirit of their now defunct *giochi d'acqua* appears to have passed into the plumbing of the neighbouring lavatories.) A tunnel between the grottoes ascends to the upper terrace with its fishpond and lawn.

To the right a path leads to a castellated 'curtain wall'. On arrival here, this turns out to be no more than the thickness of a single brick, and serves to disguise a group of greenhouses below. This fanciful illusion is of a type more common in northern Europe (one example being the castellated farmhouse at Stowe in England).

The path continues to a large parterre arranged around a single central palm, the whole bed being surrounded by festoons and swags of roses. Over to the left stands Cusani's greenhouse, splendidly assertive against its dramatic mountain background.

Turning right you return to the front of the villa. Setting off once again to the left of it, you reach the balustraded terrace which overlooks the park. This terrace runs beneath the retaining wall of the upper terrace with its machicolated watchtowers, and leads eventually to the mock-Gothic servants' quarters and stables. From here you can enter the park, whose main feature is undoubtedly the duckpond filled with ornamental waterfowl. Their eggs are clearly regarded by the local populace as a free resource.

Villa Negrotto	
Nearest major town:	Genoa
Advance booking:	No
Owner:	Comune di Arenzano
Address:	Via Sauli Pallavicino 39, Arenzano
Location:	Arenzano lies about 22 km west of Genoa on the road to Savona. The entrance to the villa is easily found from the carpark in the centre of the town.
Open:	All year 9–8, villa 9–12.30
Admission:	Free
Wheelchairs:	Yes
Refreshments:	No
Lavatories:	Yes

PALAZZO DORIA TURSI

TYPICAL GENOESE HANGING GARDEN

HISTORY

During the sixteenth century Genoa was undergoing a renaissance of its own. In 1528 the Genoese Republic had been set on a firmer footing under the rule of Admiral Andrea Doria, and the political stability that ensued resulted in a rapid expansion of the city.

At this time Genoa lacked native artists and architects of distinction. This was a not uncommon situation in such a great mercantile city, whose attentions and energies were naturally directed outwards. Exceptionally lucky in their choice, they commissioned, among others, Galeazzo Alessi who, in 1550, laid out the Strada Nuova (now Via Garibaldi). From 1558 he designed a

number of the palazzi that line it, coping brilliantly with the difficulties of the steeply sloping site. This is the earliest example in Europe of such a unified scheme of construction under a single architect.

Palazzo Doria Tursi was built in 1564 for Prince Niccolò Grimaldo. Thirty years later it passed into the hands of the Doria family, who added the loggias on either side. Since the revolution of 1848 it has belonged to the city of Genoa.

THE GARDEN

The steep hillside above the Via Garibaldi is densely covered with the buildings of Renaissance Genoa. Little space was available for gardens. Alessi and his fellow architects solved the problem by making use of the hanging garden. The result is an extraordinary interlocking pattern of buildings and gardens. In this intensely urban environment almost every window overlooks a green space, a need too often ignored by modern planners. Few of these gardens, however, have survived unchanged. The earliest to remain in its original condition, that of Palazzo Podestà, is, sadly, no longer accessible to the visitor.

Palazzo Doria Tursi's twin gardens lie on either side of the palace at the level of the *piano nobile*, and consequently overlook the street. Only the left-hand one is open to the public. On entering from the Palazzo Bianco, a small octagonal fishpond lies in front of you with a fountain of sea-horses and surrounded by pebble mosaic. Typically, statuary in these urban gardens is small in order to create an illusion of greater space than actually exists. The dwarf palms and clipped laurels surrounding the fountain build on this effect.

At the open (southern) end of the garden, overlooking the street, stand two enormous horse chestnuts. These provide shade, alleviating the heat that, in summer, is trapped between the towering limestone walls on either side. Beyond the trees runs a balustrade decorated with urns and globes of box. From here you can look straight into the first-floor windows of the palace across the road. The loggia added by the Doria family extends into the garden at this end of the palazzo. Concerts are held here in summer.

The remainder of the garden is composed of low box hedges and gravel paths. At the northern end stands the high retaining wall of the terrace above (part of the garden of the Palazzo Bianco). At its base stands a fountain, the figure of a woman whose breast spurts a fine jet of water into the pool beneath. Set against the dark green foliage with which the wall is covered, this creates a striking effect.

Left: *Palazzo Doria Tursi.*

Palazzo Doria Tursi	
Nearest major town:	Genoa
Advance booking:	No
Owner:	Municipio di Genova
Address:	Via Garibaldi 9, Genova
Location:	Via Garibaldi lies in the old town, in the centre of Genoa. The easiest way to enter is through the Galleria di Palazzo Bianco at No. 11
Open:	All year Mon–Sat, 9–1.15, 3–6; Sun, 9.15–12.45
Admission:	Free (garden only)
Wheelchairs:	No
Refreshments:	No
Lavatories:	Yes

VENETO

The region of the Veneto runs from the marshes and lagoons of Venice to the wooded hills around Verona. During the fifteenth century the rich and noble families of Venice began to reject trade as a form of investment, and to turn to the agricultural land of the Veneto as an alternative. Three hundred years of relative peace and prosperity followed. During the seventeenth and eighteenth centuries the building of villas in the Veneto became a competitive passion, best illustrated by those along the Brenta canal, each one bigger and better than the last. Sadly, little remains of the gardens that surrounded them; Villa Pisani is one of the very few exceptions.

In 1797, Napoleon put an end to the Venetian Republic and to the luxurious lifestyle that went with it. Many gardens were destroyed in the turbulent years that followed.

Despite widely differing terrain, the gardens of the Veneto do not vary greatly in style. Unlike the Romans, the Venetians were not attracted by complex architectural features. Consequently, even the gardens that were built on sloping sites, such as Barbarigo, tended to adhere to a relatively simple design. Sadly, the fact that many of them were made up of such ephemeral things as *berceaux*, pergolas and parterres means that they have disappeared without trace. Other gardens were victims to the fashion for French designs, which took hold particularly early in the low-lying areas of the Veneto.

Villa Allegri.

VILLA ALLEGRI ARVEDI

SEVENTEENTH-CENTURY VILLA AND GARDEN • EARLY
PARTERRES DE BRODERIE

HISTORY

Villa Allegri was built in 1656 for Giovanni Battista Allegri. The architect, Giovanni Battista Bianchi, built the villa on the site of an existing house, which had been the family's home since 1500.

The *parterre de broderie* below the villa is thought to date from the end of the seventeenth century. Parterre gardens were generally still being laid out in the traditional manner in Italy at this time. It was not until the eighteenth century that the French fashion for *broderie* began to take the place of square parterres divided by gravel paths. Villa

Allegri is remarkable not only as an unusually early example of the French influence on Italian garden design, but also because its elaborate layout has survived intact for nearly 300 years.

In 1824 the villa was bought by Giovanni Antonio Arvedi, and it remains in the family's

Villa Allegri: the broderie *garden.*

hands to this day. The garden is unchanged, although the *limonaia* that once stood along the left wall was demolished during the nineteenth century. A swimming pool has now taken its place, and traces of the frescoed stucco which decorated the original building cling to the wall behind the pool.

THE GARDEN

Villa Allegri is a working farm, set in the midst of a beautiful agricultural landscape. The hill that rises steeply behind the house is planted with olives, giving way to oak and hornbeam. The building is flanked by two square dovecots, to which it is linked by terraces which extend from the *piano nobile*.

The drive once extended in a straight line below the villa. During the last century its course was altered to create the informal curve that now leads up from the gatehouse. The result of the new lay-out is an unusual perspective by which one sees the villa across a charming mixture of geometrical parterre beds, topiary, fruit trees and fields. To left and right persimmons form a wide informal avenue, made particularly striking late in the year by their golden fruit. Vines grow between the trees, and box hedges and clipped cypress stand to either side of the drive.

The drive leads below the retaining wall of the terrace and into a courtyard behind the villa. The courtyard is similar to the lower garden in that it is both practical and delightfully ornamental. Flanked by stables and outhouses, it is completed by the ornate façade of the family chapel, which is still used every Sunday. It stands opposite the villa, at the top of two flights of balustraded steps and is said to have been built to commemorate San Carlo Borommeo's visit in 1542. Apparently the cardinal stopped at Cuzzano on his way to the Council of Trent – a pleasing thought, which suggests that the chapel may pre-date the villa. The niches in the retaining wall below the building once held statues. These, however, are supposed to have been destroyed by Giovanni Antonio Arvedi's daughter, Lucidalba. She had recently taken holy orders and was offended by the fact that the pagan figures stood so close to the chapel.

An ideal view of the garden is to be had from the balcony that runs along the *piano nobile*. The survival of the *parterre de broderie* bears witness to

years of dedicated care by the Arvedi. Low box hedges create a swirling and complex design which is punctuated by large cones of clipped box. The edge of the garden is decorated with lemon trees in pots. Earlier in this century roses were planted among the *broderie* beds. Now, however, the garden has been restored to its original form by the present owner and is beautifully maintained by only two gardeners.

Villa Allegri Arvedi	
Nearest major town:	Verona
Advance booking:	Yes
Owner:	Sig. Ottavio Arvedi
Address:	Cuzzano
Location:	Cuzzano is approx 11 km north of Verona. From the city centre, follow signs for the ss11 to Vicenza. On the outskirts of Verona you will see signs for Grezzana. Taking turning for 'Grezzana centro'. The villa is on hillside above the road. (NB: although they appear very close on the map, allow plenty of time if you decide to go cross country between Villa Allegri and Villa Rizzardi.)
Open:	Strictly by appointment – letter or telephone.
Admission:	Free
Wheelchairs:	No
Refreshments:	No
Lavatories:	No

VILLA BARBARIGO
VILLA DONÀ DELLE ROSE

LATE SEVENTEENTH-CENTURY GARDEN • RABBIT ISLAND

HISTORY

The Barbarigo were an illustrious Venetian family who had bought some of the marshy land near Valsanzibio. In 1631 they exiled themselves to the country to escape an outbreak of plague in Venice. It was at this point that they began to make plans to build a new villa. It was not until 1669, however, that Antonio Barbarigo, who was to become Procurator of St Marks, gave orders for building work to begin.

The garden evolved over many decades. Documents preserved in the Museo Correr in Venice serve as a record of its progress over the years. A map drawn in 1678 shows the work well advanced but by no means complete. In the same year payment was made for iron supports for the statues. In 1694 a building was demolished to make way for a further extension to the layout. In 1717 the Barbarigo bought additional land, thus securing rights over the little stream and drainage canal that were to feed the pools and fountains of the garden.

Villa Barbarigo soon became famous for its magnificent flower garden. During the seventeenth century the green garden of the early Renaissance had been largely abandoned in Italy. The Barbarigo were evidently enthralled by the new fashion for rare plants, some of them imported from as far afield as India and the Americas. Paolo Bartolomeo Clarici, whose book, *Istoria e coltura delle piante*, was published in Venice in 1702, was particularly impressed by the double stocks. He listed 233 different plants in the garden, and 226 different kinds of fruit.

During the Second World War the villa narrowly escaped destruction when the avenue above it was bombed. The trees have been replanted by the present owners.

The property eventually passed out of the Barbarigo family to the Donà delle Rose. It now belongs to the Pizzoni Ardemani.

THE GARDEN

Before entering the garden it is well worth walking the few yards down the road to the watergate. It is said that the pool that lies between the gate and the road was once a part of the web of canals that covered this area, linking Valsanzibio to Venice. If this was the case, the Barbarigo's guests would have seen the garden for the first time from the level of the watergate, and it is right that we should share their experience. It may be, of course, that the gate was never used, and that it was designed simply for the enjoyment of passersby, who could pause to admire the pools and cascades that descend the gentle slope behind it. The creation of views through a boundary wall dates back to the fifteenth century in the Veneto, and should not be confused with the French fashion for *clairvoyées*.

The watergate is dedicated entirely to the *terra firma* sport of hunting. Diana stands on the broken arch of the pediment with her dogs. The entire structure is decorated with bas-reliefs of game that has been successfully caught and is already neatly hung: deer, bears, foxes, hares and wild boar are all accurately portrayed alongside the paraphernalia of the chase.

The contemporary visitor enters the garden through the base of an unfinished tower in the boundary wall, and emerges in an area of eighteenth-century woodland. The garden is contained in a natural amphitheatre in the Euganean hills. The two intersecting vistas that form its core are designed to lead the eye up to the wooded slopes that enclose the site on all sides. Consequently, one is always aware of the magnificence of its setting.

The first vista is created by the two pools which lie on the gentle slope above the watergate. The first is presided over by two enormous bearded sea gods, who lie against its rough retaining wall. The angle of the slope is such that the other pool is all but invisible from the watergate. Box hedges, 12

Villa Barbarigo: the watergate.

50

feet high, enclose the area on both sides. Between the pools four delightfully mischievous putti sit dangling their feet in their own circular pond.

The garden's second axis crosses the first immediately above the pools. It consists of a *tapis vert* which runs the length of the site. When we were there, a gardener equipped with an enormously long wooden ladder and a plumb line was clipping the huge box hedges that flank the *tapis vert* and serve to frame the villa which stands at its far end. The vista is extended by means of a cypress avenue, cutting through the trees on the slope above the villa.

At the far end of the *tapis vert* steps lead up to the bright parterres and beautiful topiary of the private garden in front of the villa. Each step is inscribed with verses which describe the garden as a kind of private paradise: sun and moon shine brightly, Mars lays down his weapons, death is powerless and tears have no place. The images are those of an earlier period, far removed from the unsettled universe that dominated the baroque imagination and infiltrated the gardens of the age.

A massive statue of Father Time, bent beneath the weight of his load, stands in a clearing in the *bosco* between the stables and the watergate. He was undoubtedly part of a wider symbolic theme which is largely lost to our modern imaginations.

One of the most delightful features of the garden is the rabbit island which lies in a clearing in the *bosco*. The island is encircled by a moat, and can only be reached by means of a wooden drawbridge. Worn statues of rabbits stand at the water's edge, and at the centre of the island there is a rustic stone tower which supports an ornate aviary. The white doves that inhabit it are oblivious to a realistic stone hawk that hovers over them.

The peace of this delightful garden is occasionally shattered by the arrival of the owner's passionately friendly Airedales.

Villa Barbarigo (Villa Donà delle Rose)

Nearest major town:	Padua
Advance booking:	No
Owner:	Count Pizzoni Ardemani
Address:	Valsanzibio
Location:	Valsanzibio is approx. 18 km south of Padua. Follow signs for the ss16 to Monselice from the centre of Padua. After approx 15 km turn off to Battaglia Terme. Drive through the town and cross the railway. Valsanzibio is signposted left almost immediately. Villa signposted from the village.
Open:	15 Mar–15 Nov, 10–12, 2–5.30. Closed Mon mornings
Admission:	L4500
Wheelchairs:	No
Refreshments:	No
Lavatories:	No

CASTELLO DEL CATAIO

UNIQUE GOTHIC CASTLE • SIXTEENTH-CENTURY AND EARLY NINETEENTH-CENTURY GARDENS

HISTORY

The extraordinary collection of buildings that make up the castle of Cataio date back to 1570. However, their Gothic style makes them an anomaly in Italian architecture of the sixteenth century.

Pius Aeneas I degli Obizzi employed Andrea della Valle to design the main building. It was built on the site of an existing family villa, already known as Cataio after the hill on which it was built. Edith Wharton suggests that the design was based on the plans, brought back by Marco Polo, of a castle in Tartary. Whatever the source of his inspiration, della Valle certainly created a fitting home for Obizzi, who was a distinguished man at arms in the Venetian army. Almost stranger than the design itself is the fact that it took only three years to build.

Obizzi's nephew, Pius Aeneas II, inherited Cataio in 1648. He was impassioned about it, and spent the next eighteen years extending the building and laying out magnificent gardens. However, he never employed an architect, believing that he was the only person capable of truly understanding the site.

Tommaso was the last of the Obizzi, and when he died, at the beginning of the nineteenth century, he left Cataio to the Duke of Modena. It

then passed to the Habsburgs, who extended it, made it into a summer residence, and took the Obizzi collection of paintings and sculptures with them to Vienna.

The Habsburgs sold the castle to the dalla Francesca family. The three dalla Francesca sisters, who had an unfortunate reputation for miserliness, set up a business for growing and drying tobacco. None of them married, and when the last sister died, in 1986, the property was inherited by three different families.

When we saw Cataio its future was uncertain. The heirs had decided to sell it, and it was said that it might well be bought by the State.

THE GARDEN

The creation of the gardens at Cataio cannot have been an easy task. The castle was built against a steep hill, and the grounds were bounded on one side by the Brenta canal. Despite these difficulties, Pius Aeneas II built an extraordinary number of different gardens. The site dictated that many of them should take the form of terraces and hanging gardens. During the nineteenth century, his gardens above the Brenta were compared to the Hanging Gardens of Babylon. Additional terraces

Castello del Cataio.

were wedged between the castle walls and the hill that rises up behind it. Fountains, *giochi d'acqua*, courtyards, ramps and passages added to the fascination of the eccentric layout.

Sadly, we have seen merely a fraction of all that Cataio has to offer. We were only allowed into the garden that lies on the level ground below the castle's south wall. If the property is bought by the State, it is likely that the public will be given access to the rest of the grounds – and we will be among the first visitors!

This part of the garden was originally laid out around two balustraded fishponds, decorated with orange trees in pots. According to a contemporary description, pergolas once surrounded the garden, clematis and jasmine hung in swags from the retaining wall below the drive, and there was a *bosco* planted with elm and containing a maze.

The existing garden bears little resemblance to Pius Aeneas's seventeenth-century creation. The layout, which was probably designed for Tommaso Obizzi, dates from the early nineteenth century. Much as we dislike linking neglect with the idea of romance in a garden, it cannot be denied that the passage of years has turned this into a wild and romantic place, despite the struggles of the single gardener employed to maintain it.

A long walk, lined from end to end with pots of citrus fruit and flowering geraniums, runs the width of the garden. The greenhouses, which are concealed from the drive by a neo-Gothic façade, stand at one end. At the other, steps lead up to the raised drive immediately in front of the castle's main entrance. The jasmine and clematis of the seventeenth century have been ousted by climbing roses.

The rest of the garden is divided between a lake, which may have replaced the fishponds of the earlier layout, and a wooded area. The magnificent magnolias that surround the lake are known to have been planted by Tommaso Obizzi in 1803. Low box hedges stand to either side of the path that runs by the water's edge. At the far end of the lake, weeping willows screen a view of the castle across the water.

The wood which covers the rest of the site is divided by a series of parallel avenues, walks and beech tunnels. The principal avenue leads to a cenotaph, erected by Tommaso Obizzi in memory of his wife. The area between the avenue and the lake was once a web of little paths. These are now, for the most part, impassable. However, determined explorers may find the swimming pool, which must date from the beginning of this century, and the derelict bathing hut. The pool can only be reached by walking through the remains of the small maze, which, no doubt, guaranteed the privacy of the bathers.

Castello del Cataio	
Nearest major town:	Padua
Advance booking:	No
Owner:	Dalla Francesca family
Address:	Battaglia Terme
Location:	Battaglia Terme is approx. 16 km south west of Padua. From Padua take the A13 motorway towards Ferrara. Take the Terme Euganee exit. Cataio stands on the ss16 to Battaglia. This gate is locked, so go into Battaglia, turning right over the canal. Take the first turning right below the embankment road (ignoring sign saying private road). Road leads between fields and houses. Turn right again onto dirt track leading towards the castle.
Open:	Apply to gardener in the house to left of back entrance.
Admission:	Free
Wheelchairs:	No
Refreshments:	No
Lavatories:	No

VILLA DELLA TORRE

SIXTEENTH-CENTURY VILLA AND GARDEN IN CLASSICAL ROMAN STYLE

HISTORY

Giulio della Torre came into possession of the land on which the villa is built through his marriage in 1504. Although we do not know exactly when building work began, it has been established that it was not finished by the time of his death in 1547. A map of 1562, however, shows the villa complete.

Della Torre was a classical scholar and it was fitting that his home should imitate the Roman villas that fired his imagination. Consequently, the house is built around a colonnaded peristyle which once enclosed a garden.

After Giulio's death the property passed to his son Girolamo, and from him to Marcantonio della Torre. During Marcantonio's lifetime it became a meeting place for his cultured and influential friends. It is to this era that we owe the delightful verses of the Venetian poet Veronica Franco. Her poems pay tribute not only to the garden, but also to the gardener who tended it.

Very little documentary evidence has survived regarding the villa's early history. The name of the architect has never been finally established, although it is generally attributed to Giulio Romano. The fireplaces inside the villa, which are set within the gaping jaws of grotesque masks, seem to correspond with Romano's bizarre sense of humour. Cristoforo Sorte is said to have been responsible for the complex system by which water was brought to the garden from afar.

Villa della Torre is badly in need of restoration. We were relieved to hear that its present owners, the Cazzola family, were about to take this in hand.

Villa della Torre: the peristyle.

THE GARDEN

The villa stands against the side of a steep hill in the Valpolicella. Its isolated position and the unsettled times in which they lived explain the della Torre family's decision to enclose their garden within a high boundary wall. The original entrance was at the bottom of the lower garden. Lawns, intersected by four paths and decorated with a central fountain, once filled the space that is now taken up by a vineyard. Today, one enters the garden at the level of the terrace in front of the villa. It is linked to the lower garden by four flights of steps. Beneath the steps there is a grotto. A striking oblong pool, spanned by a triple-arched bridge, stands at the centre of the terrace. The aviary on the far wall would once have been full of songbirds, just as the pool was once full of fish.

Like the villas of ancient Rome, Villa della Torre had a garden that was laid out on a single axis. The climax of its four-part design was created by the courtyard garden in the colonnaded peristyle of the house. By standing at the centre of the courtyard, one could look across the bridge that spanned the pool, down the path that divided the lower garden and through the entrance at its far end. Behind the villa the vista was extended by an avenue that climbed the slope beyond the boundaries of the enclosed garden.

The villa's principal rooms open into the colonnades that surround the courtyard. When the doors were open, the courtyard would have served simply as another room in the house. This fusion between house and garden was also inspired by Roman designs.

In architectural terms, the courtyard represents a somewhat eccentric interpretation of the original. However, to appreciate the effect that Giulio della Torre wished to achieve, one must imagine the space filled with magnificent pots of orange and lemon trees, and alive with the sound of the water that ran from the fountain and the grotesques to each side of the doors. The niches under the shady colonnades are now empty, but they once held the statues of pagan figures. At night the walls would have leapt with the shadows thrown by burning torches held in the sconces.

If the courtyard is to be seen as a Roman garden, the area behind the villa resembles a *hortus conclusus*. It is sheltered by high walls and much of the space is taken up by cherry trees, apples, pears and persimmons. A swing hangs from one of the trees, and rough grass and wild flowers grow between them. A flight of steps runs up the central axis to a low terrace that bounds the garden on all sides. One side of the terrace is given up to a bowling alley, and the family chapel stands in the opposite corner. The bell tower is decorated with curious brick battlements, matching those that crown the boundary wall of the terrace in front of the villa. The garden is full of the sound of birdsong and the bleating of the sheep that scramble about on the hillside above.

Villa della Torre	
Nearest major town:	Verona
Advance booking:	Yes
Owner:	Dottore Gianantonio Cazzola
Address:	Fumane
Location:	Fumane is approx. 22 km north west of Verona. Take the ss12 for Trento from Verona, turning off it at Parona, after approx. 6 km. Turn off this road towards Negrar, and then follow signs for Fumane. The villa is on the far side of the village, and can be recognised by the chapel's crenellated bell tower. The entrance is a dirt track beyond the boundary wall, leading into the farmyard.
Open:	Strictly by appointment. Telephone/write to owner, either at the villa or at his address in Verona.
Admission:	Free
Wheelchairs:	No
Refreshments:	No
Lavatories:	No

GIARDINO GIUSTI

DELIGHTFUL SIXTEENTH-CENTURY GARDEN IN CENTRAL VERONA

HISTORY

The Giusti were originally a Tuscan family. They came to Verona at the beginning of the fifteenth century and bought property beneath the hill of San Zeno, just beyond the city boundaries. Nobody knows whether their full title of Giusti del Giardino acted as a kind of self-fulfilling prophecy, or whether, more probably, it dates from the creation of the garden that was to become famous all over Europe.

Count Agostino Giusti – a powerful figure in the political and cultural life of Verona – had the gardens laid out at some point between 1565 and 1580. The architect's name is unknown, and none of the original plans survive. Over the centuries, however, numerous visitors have depicted and described the garden, which was open to the public from the moment of its creation. Volkamer's

engraving of 1714 shows a pool occupying the south-eastern section of the lower garden. It was rather like the pool at Villa Lante, with an island linked to the garden by a bridge. A statue of Venus, thought to have been by Alessandro Vittoria, stood at the centre of the island. We know that this delightful feature survived at least until the nineteenth century, as it is included in the official records of 1830.

During Agostino Giusti's lifetime the garden was often used as a setting for plays and concerts. In 1581 Tasso's *Aminta* was staged here for the third time. It is said that the mouth of the grotesque mask on the cliff face was made to spit fire for the occasion, and strange music issued from one of the grottoes.

In 1611 the English traveller Thomas Coryat

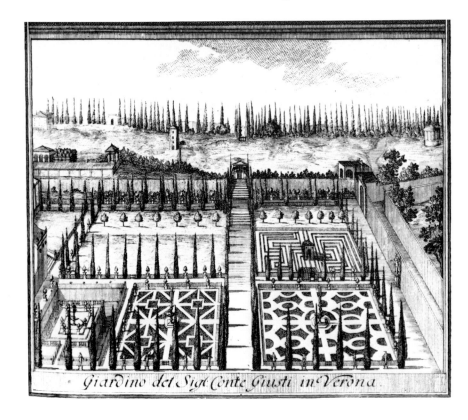

Giardino Giusti. Continuation der Nurnbergischen Hesperidum, *Volkamer, 1788. (Bodleian, Vet. D4.c.11)*

Giardino del Sig.ᵗ Conte Giusti in Verona.

visited 'Count Augustus Justus', and was shown round the garden. He described it as 'a passing delectable place of solace, beautified with many curious knots, fruits of divers sorts and two rowes of lofty cypresse trees, three and thirty in ranke'.

In 1615 Agostino died and his son Giovan Giacomo Giusti inherited the property. In 1621 he was granted permission to convey water to the garden from a nearby stream. As a result he built additional fountains of a more complex design, and installed various *giochi d'acqua*. Previously, rainwater, collected in a large underground cistern beneath a well in the upper garden, had been the sole water supply.

The garden belongs to the Giusti family to this day. However, continuity of ownership – which has so often protected the original layout of a garden – has not been entirely effective in this case. When Georgina Masson saw it she complained of the inappropriate landscaping of the slope below the cliff.

THE GARDEN

The garden is built on two levels which are linked by a spiral staircase. The lower garden lies on the same level as the villa. It is enclosed on three sides by walls, made up, in part, of the remains of the city's fortifications. A sheer cliff face forms the northern boundary. The upper garden lies on a narrow shelf at the top of the cliff.

A high wall separates the garden from the arcaded entrance of the palazzo. A wrought-iron gate let into the centre of the wall allows passersby to enjoy a glimpse of the garden from the street. The gate is on an axis with the famous cypress avenue that has provoked the wonder of successive generations of visitors. The massive trees create striped shadows, seeming to reflect the lines of the steps that link the avenue to the base of the cliff. There is a hideous mask hewn out of the rough face of the cliff above the steps. Its teeth are bared in fury at the unsuspecting visitors who lean over the balustrade of the belvedere that is built above its head. Its design is reminiscent of the grotto in the Sacro Bosco in Bomarzo, and of the curious fireplaces at Villa della Torre (page 55).

Volkamer's print suggests that the garden may originally have been laid out as a series of garden 'rooms' to either side of the avenue. Perhaps it was on account of their Tuscan origins that the Giusti chose a design that had so much more in common with the gardens of central Italy than with those of the Veneto. To the east this layout has been preserved. A row of cypresses acts as a screen, dividing the garden in two. The first 'room' is filled with green parterres. They are arranged around a simple fountain where water and weeds combine to delightful effect. Female statues stand among the cypresses that bound the garden on all sides. Many of the Roman tombstones, which were collected by Agostino and Gian Giacomo Giusti, still stand about in this part of the garden.

In his diary of 1736, Président de Brosses records a nasty experience in the Giardino Giusti: 'I got lost in a maze, and I was an hour wandering in the blazing sun, and would have still been there, had I not been taken out by one of the people of the place'. The maze still stands behind the cypress screen, just as it does in Volkamer's print of 1714. It was redesigned by Luigi Trezza in 1786.

The left-hand portion of the lower garden is also divided by cypresses. They were planted six years ago in order to restore the original layout, and are still too small to create a screen. Consequently, the sweep of the box parterres, which climb the slope below the cliff, can be enjoyed from the bottom of the garden. The beds are divided by gravel paths decorated with lemon trees in pots. Each bed is made up of a complex combination of interlocking shapes, rather like the parts of a puzzle. The pale statues that grace the parterres stand out against the rich greens of cypress and box.

The ancient city wall creates the boundary of this side of the garden. It used to serve as the rear wall of the *limonaia*, which was decorated with statues of Ceres, Bacchus and Venus by Lorenzo Muttoni. These still stand in their original positions along the wall.

The steps at the end of the avenue mark the transition between the formal and the wild sections of the garden. Terraces originally extended to either side of them, and were planted with fig trees, oranges, lemons and apricots.

A classical portal forms the entrance to the grotto at the top of the steps. Little remains, however, of its fabulous interior. The walls were once covered with conch shells, coral, mother-of-pearl, painted glass and pebbles. Some of this decoration can still be seen on the ceiling. Landscapes painted in the niches on the walls to right and left seemed to transform the grotto into an open loggia. Traces of the painted stucco cling to the wall just inside the entrance. A pair of mirrors used to be set into the far wall, creating the illusion that another, identical garden lay beyond.

Four other grottoes were let into the cliff at different levels. There was one above the maze, built in such a way that it amplified and distorted sound. Another, which can still be seen at the foot of the tower that links the lower and upper gardens, served as the family chapel.

A winding path leads up the wooded slope, passing at one point through a pergola and at another through a charming open loggia, to emerge eventually at the foot of the tower built against the cliff face. The worn spiral staircase that leads up through the tower is the only link between the two levels of the garden.

Rare vegetables and scented herbs were once planted on the undulating site of the upper garden. A circular temple, demolished in 1920, stood to the east, and the Palazzina di Venere, or Little Palace of Venus, formed its boundary to the west. From the belvedere there is a magnificent view down the avenue and across Verona.

Giardino Giusti	
Nearest major town:	Verona
Advance booking:	No
Owner:	Conte Giusti del Giardino
Address:	Via Giardino Giusti 2
Location:	Follow signs for Giardino Giusti from the centre of Verona.
Open:	Dawn to dusk. Closed Mon
Admission:	Adults L4000, children L2000 (garden only)
Wheelchairs:	Yes, in lower garden
Refreshments:	No
Lavatories:	Yes

Left: *Giardino Giusti: the lower garden.*

Right: *Giardino Giusti.*

VILLA MARCELLO

BEAUTIFULLY MAINTAINED SIXTEENTH-CENTURY GARDEN

HISTORY

Villa Marcello was built for the Marcello family in 1580. All the documents concerning its early history were destroyed during the Second World War.

During the nineteenth century, additions were made to the back of the main building. The arcades were also built at the front at this time.

During the First World War the villa was commandeered by the German Army and used as a military base. Apart from this brief interlude, it has been in the hands of the Marcello family ever since it was built.

THE GARDEN

The sixteenth-century garden lies behind the villa. It consists of a *bosco*, a canal and a long rectangular pool. The *bosco* is made up of beech, plane and poplar, planted in a series of long walks and avenues. Sixteenth-century Venetian statues stand in the dappled shade at the end of each avenue. Originally, the area between the avenues was planted with fruit trees. A sixteenth-century dovecot stands at the far end of the central avenue, on an axis with the villa. It is a substantial building of several storeys. During the First World War it housed carrier pigeons, and the room below the tower served as the office from which they were despatched. After the war the building was used for breeding silkworms.

The rear wall of the villa is decorated with a series of charming statues depicting monkey musicians. The monkeys are only just over a foot high, and stand on a series of pillars. There are seven of them in all, one with cymbals, another playing a concertina, and the others joining in on the violin, tambourine, pan-pipes and banjo. The conductor stands at the centre with baton raised.

The pool lies directly behind the villa, creating a striking perspective from the *piano nobile*. It is flanked by gnarled beech tunnels, and at the far end the eye is stopped by a simple brick wall ornamented with putti. Closer examination reveals that they are holding sheaves of corn, flowers and

Above: *Villa Marcello: Venice defeated.*

Right: *Villa Marcello: the pool.*

grapes. There is a curious collection of statues standing along the boundary wall of the garden. A bridled Venetian lion represents Venice conquered by the Austrians. It is strange that this should have been allowed to survive after the liberation of the Veneto.

The pool is fed by a canal which leads in from the fields. It was originally dug to obtain the clay that was needed to make bricks for building the villa. When its practical use was over, it was made into one of the decorative features of the garden. It is shaded by trees, and a series of sixteenth-century Venetian dwarves stand along its banks. Statues of dwarves are very common in the Veneto, but these seem unusually grotesque.

In front of the villa there is a formal garden laid out in the Italian manner. Large green parterres divided by gravel walks are arranged around a central fountain. These were planted after the Second World War, replacing a nineteenth-century layout. The paths that wind through the trees to either side of the parterres are its only remaining feature. In one of the trees there is a magnificent tree house – not an original construction!

We were shown round by the owner's charming eleven-year-old son. His enthusiasm for the garden and its history suggests that it will be looked after as beautifully in the future as it is today.

Villa Marcello	
Nearest major town:	Padua
Advance booking:	Yes
Owner:	Conte Vettore Marcello
Address:	Levada di Piombino Dese
Location:	From Padua take the ss307 for Castelfranco. After about 25 km turn right in Resana for Levada. The villa is unmistakable on the left just through Levada
Open:	Organised groups only. Write or phone in advance
Admission:	Free
Wheelchairs:	Yes
Refreshments:	No
Lavatories:	No

VILLA PISANI
VILLA IMPERIALE, VILLA NAZIONALE

EIGHTEENTH-CENTURY GARDEN IN THE FRENCH MANNER
• MAZE • MOATED COFFEE-HOUSE

HISTORY

Alvise Pisani was the Venetian ambassador to Paris between 1699 and 1704, and Louis XIV was god-father to his son. In 1711 he became Procurator of St Marks, and in 1735 he was elected Doge of Venice. It is fitting that the villa designed for him by Francesco Maria Preti should be the largest and most elaborate on the Brenta.

For almost twenty years Alvise and his brother Almorò had been planning to demolish the simple sixteenth-century family residence and replace it with something more elaborate. Girolamo Frigimelica had been commissioned to draw up plans for a new villa and garden in 1719. The existing building was duly demolished in 1720, but Frigimelica's plans for its replacement were never executed. His design for the gardens was retained, however, and when the villa was built in 1735 it had to be fitted into the space that Frigimelica had originally left for it.

Villa Pisani stayed in the family until 1807, when Napoleon ordered that it should be bought by the kingdom of Italy. He spent one night there him-self, and then presented it to his viceroy Eugène Beauharnais, thus initiating its role in public life.

During the reorganisation that followed the Napoleonic period, Austria was granted possession of the Veneto. For the first 30 years of Austrian rule, the villa and its grounds were completely neglected. In 1849, however, it became a military hospital, and some restoration work was initiated. In 1882 it was declared a national monument.

During the early years of this century the villa was privately managed with the aid of a State sub-sidy. After the Second World War the property reverted to State ownership. Lack of staff and funding reduced the building and its grounds to such a critical condition that it had to be closed in 1979. Thankfully, restoration work is now underway. However, Frigimelica's splendid garden is badly scarred by more than a hundred years of neglect.

THE GARDEN

As they alighted from their boat, Alvise Pisani's visitors would have been able to look through the massive portico of the villa and along the central perspective of the garden. Today the north–south perspective is created by a sheet of water which runs the length of the garden. Originally, the entire space was filled with *parterres de broderie*. In 1911 they were torn out to make way for the pool, which was then used for testing naval scale models. At the time this was undoubtedly an act of vandal-ism, however one cannot fail to appreciate the effect of the still water stretching away from the villa, and the reflection of the beautiful façade of Frigimelica's stable block, which has survived to

Villa Pisani: the central pool, with the stable block.

create a focus for the central axis of the garden. As an *habitué* of the French court, Pisani would have been familiar with the work of Le Nôtre. He may have encouraged Frigimelica to adopt some of the Frenchman's ideas, which were becoming increasingly fashionable in Italy at that time. Whether influenced by Le Nôtre or not, Frigimelica's decision to base his design around a series of avenues was certainly appropriate to the flat site.

The three sections that made up the original garden still form the basis of its layout. To either side of the parterres Frigimelica planted areas of *bosco* intersected by avenues. These avenues created vistas which ran the length of the garden. Additional avenues radiated out from the vertical axis, and were aligned in such a way that they led the eye across the parterres and through the trees beyond. The doors and windows that pierce the boundary wall allowed these vistas to extend beyond the garden and into the countryside that surrounded the villa.

It is in the right-hand portion of the garden that the original design can best be seen. The magnificent maze is to be found at the end of a long lime avenue. Its entrance is flanked by two laughing putti, witnesses to the desperation of many an illustrious guest lost among the 6 foot hedges within. Pisani himself could watch their efforts from the delightful tower at the centre of the maze, which he would have climbed by means of the ornate spiral staircase that encircles it. The statue of Minerva that crowns the tower may be an allusion to the difficulty of attaining wisdom.

Frigimelica's curious hexagonal arch is to be found in the middle of the *bosco*, at the centre of six radiating avenues. Worn stone steps spiral up through the building and emerge onto a balustraded terrace. From this vantage point one can look down the avenues in all directions. However, the trees have reached such a height that one's view of the garden may not be as comprehensive as Frigimelica intended. The *limonaie* run away from the arch to left and right. There was a time when they sheltered 66 varieties of citrus trees. When the villa belonged to the Pisani as many as 20,000 lemons were sold each year. Until the mid-nineteenth century, prize-winning camellias continued to be grown in the hothouses at the villa.

Frigimelica's coffee-house stands on a mound which used to be planted with hedges clipped into the form of flights of steps. During the nineteenth century the hedges were lost, tall trees were planted around the site, and the moat was dug as part of a new drainage system.

The *bosco* to the left of the villa was originally divided up into five distinct areas by a series of avenues. Each area was slightly different: one consisted of a lawn with a central statue, another was characterised by box hedges, and the one furthest from the villa was filled with paths which wound their way through the trees to a little mound. Most of this part of the garden was destroyed during the nineteenth century. Here, as elsewhere in the garden, the trees are in a poor and untended state.

With a little effort it is almost always possible to imagine villas and their gardens back into real life, even when they have not been lived in for many years. We were sad to find that Villa Pisani had an air of desertion that could not be overcome by any feat of the imagination.

Villa Pisani (Villa Imperiale, Villa Nazionale)	
Nearest major town:	Padua
Advance booking:	No
Owner:	State
Address:	Strà
Location:	Strà is approx. 8 km east of Padua. Leave Padua on the ss11 for Venice. The villa and carpark are on the left of the road just beyond Strà.
Open:	9–5.30. Closed Mon
Admission:	L3000, villa and gardens
Wheelchairs:	Yes
Refreshments:	No
Lavatories:	Yes

PRATO DELLA VALLE

UNUSUAL LATE EIGHTEENTH-CENTURY PUBLIC GARDEN

HISTORY

Prato della Valle was the name given to a field in the middle of Padua. It was too boggy for permanent buildings, and plagued by annual flooding. The ancient Romans had used it as a burial ground; later on it became a site for fairs and markets.

When Andrea Memmo became Governor of Padua in 1775, he recognised the political advantage to be gained by solving the age-old problem of the Prato. The subject was topical at the time, following a particularly severe flood.

Memmo's motives were not purely political. He had a genuine desire to create something that would bring pleasure to the citizens of Padua. He wanted to give them a garden so unusual that visitors would be drawn from all over Europe to see it. He hoped that these visitors would provide the city with a new source of income. Memmo extended the idea of mixing pleasure and commerce by suggesting that there should be shops in the garden.

Domenico Cerato was commissioned to help Memmo by drawing up the plans for the project. Between them they created a striking design which has been preserved by the civic museum in Padua. Their idea was to dig an oval canal in the centre of the site, using the earth from the excavation to make a raised island. The canal was to be fed by water drained off from the rest of the field. It was

Prato della Valle.

64

an ingenious idea, providing a neat solution both to the problem of flooding and to the need to give form and focus to the irregular site.

Cerato's plan and the structure of the island today are identical in all but two respects. A portico was to be built around the perimeter of the island to house the shops. Part of it was to be a permanent structure supported by stone columns, and the rest was to be made of marbled wood. In the event, the excessive cost of draining the area and the scepticism of local tradesmen combined to persuade Memmo to drop the portico from the plans. The failure of the commercial aspect of the plan was a severe blow for Memmo. It altered the garden's place within the life of the city, cutting it off from daily life and turning it into a place reserved for pleasure and repose.

The site of four structures described as *berceaux* was marked on the original plans. Cerato's notes stipulate that these should be Chinese in appearance, and decorated with a black and white pattern. An engraving of 1786 by Francesco Piranesi shows the *berceaux* in place – looking more like striped tents!

Cerato's plan shows the canal lined, as it is today, by innumerable statues. Executed by local artists and outsiders, the statues were all donations. The first to be produced depicted Cicero. This outraged the citizens of Padua, who felt that a Roman, however worthy, could not be given a place of honour in their city. Following this incident it was announced that the statues had to represent famous people or heroes who had been linked in some way to the city or its university. Curiously, no saints were allowed. In all 78 figures were produced over a period of about 60 years.

THE GARDEN
The urban designers of this century have made no concessions to the Prato della Valle, using its perimeter as a massive roundabout. However, the raised island and canal flanked by statues are still instantly recognisable amid the cars.

Four bridges span the canal and lead to the broad walks which intersect the island to meet at its centre. Impressive bishops with copes and mitres preside over two of the bridges, stretching out their hands in benediction. The stone benches that stand around the central 'piazza' (so named by Cerato), and the urns on pedestals that decorate

the walks were all included in the original plan.

The plane trees were planted during the nineteenth century. Overcrowding and disease detract from their beauty and, far from adorning the site, they obscure the bold lines of Cerato's design.

The statues are a marvellous sight. Most of them were executed by artists whose names have now sunk into obscurity. One of them, however, is attributed to Antonio Canova. Each statue stands on a pedestal inscribed in Latin with the name and credentials of the subject.

Prato della Valle	
Nearest major town:	Padua
Advance booking:	No
Owner:	Comune di Padova
Address:	Padua
Location:	Prato della Valle is next to the Oratorio di San Giorgio in the centre of Padua. Follow signs to S. Giorgio. Parking off Viale Carducci/ Via 58 Fanteria.
Open:	Always
Admission:	Free
Wheelchairs:	Yes
Refreshments:	No
Lavatories:	No

VILLA RIZZARDI

BEAUTIFULLY MAINTAINED SIXTEENTH-CENTURY GARDEN IN RURAL SETTING

HISTORY

The garden of Villa Rizzardi was laid out on the eve of the period in which *giardini all'italiana* were swept away, making space for those expanses of grass and woodland known as 'English' parks. The knowledge that it was the last garden of its kind to be created in Italy makes the perfectly maintained layout of Villa Rizzardi particularly precious.

The garden was designed for Count Antonio Rizzardi by Luigi Trezza, and laid out between 1783 and 1791. However, the plans for the 'green theatre' were not finalised until 1796.

The Rizzardi were a Veronese family whose wealth derived from foreign trade. Consequently, they were unusually well placed to comply with the fashion of the day by filling their garden with strange and wonderful plants imported from abroad.

The property still belongs to the Rizzardi. The villa was rebuilt during the nineteenth century, and is at present rented to a Spanish sculptor whose works stand about the lower garden.

THE GARDEN

The gardens lie on a slope above the villa. They are set out to create three distinct levels. On a first visit the simplicity of this layout is not immediately apparent. By screening the view between the different levels, and distracting the visitor with glimpses of the hills beyond the garden, Trezza succeeded in concealing the basis of his design. It is only when you arrive at the cypress avenue that runs across the garden, intersecting each of its three levels, that you understand the design, and perceive the true proportions of the garden which, until that moment, seems limitless.

One enters the garden today at its highest level. A path flanked by ancient hornbeams leads to the *bosco*, which used to be planted with oaks. During the Austrian occupation of the Veneto many of these were felled, however the yew and beech that replaced them create a highly effective 'wild' area within the garden. The trees throw deep shadows, half-concealing the humped forms of stone pumas that crouch to either side of the path. Perhaps the *bosco* should be seen as a substitute for the 'enclosure for wild beasts' that Pietro de Crescenzi advocated for the gardens of kings and noblemen in the fourteenth century. Miniature palms are all that remain of the mixture of indigenous and exotic plants that once carpeted the area, and no doubt reminded Count Rizzardi of the real jungles that he had seen on his travels.

The *bosco* also conceals a 'Roman' ruin. The circular building was once surrounded by a box hedge from which other hedges radiated like the points of a star. The boughs of the beech trees that meet high above it create the building's roof, and fill it with soft, dappled light. The inside walls are decorated with stalactites that were collected from all over the Valpolicella. Niches between the doors contain statues – one of Diana and another of Hercules, each in violent combat with a wild beast.

Emerging from the *bosco* you arrive at the midpoint of the cypress avenue that climbs the slope, intersecting the walks that mark each level of the garden. At the top of the slope there is a charming belvedere, embraced by two flights of steps. Putti stand on the octagonal balustrade that surrounds the terrace, overlooking a vista that runs the length of the avenue, only to be stopped by the cypresses that are grouped around a statue of Minerva at its far end. Trezza no doubt intended that the belvedere should offer views over the surrounding countryside, unobscured by the trees that have now outgrown their intended height. The custodian's youngest daughter keeps house among the cypresses at the top of the avenue – we saw her disappearing among their leaves like the *genius loci*.

Trezza's 'green theatre', often described as the finest in Italy, lies to one side of the avenue. It is linked to the villa by a second avenue, which also serves to mark the second level of the garden. The theatre was the last of the garden's features to be

laid out, a fact that can be explained by Trezza's determination to find an ideal site for it. Audiences at the concerts that are held here each summer reap the rewards of his care – the acoustics are perfect.

Trezza looked to the amphitheatres of ancient Greece for his inspiration. The auditorium consists of seven tiers of turf seats, intersected by three flights of steps. Like the cypresses at the end of the avenue, the box hedges that separate the tiers have outgrown their purpose, making the seats unusable. However, a thousand people can be accommodated in the space below the stage. The beech hedge that encloses the theatre has been clipped to create niches for Pietro Muttoni's classical statues. Each one is marked by a dome on the top of the hedge – a particularly delightful detail. The raised stage is over 30 yards wide, with flats and a backdrop made of clipped beech. The space

between the stage and the high beech hedge that surrounds the theatre served as changing rooms. The stone benches that stand in the wings were presumably provided for those overcome by stagefright.

The lowest level of the garden is marked by an alley of elm. The trees are pleached to a height of 20 feet. Rather than allowing them to meet and form a tunnel, the design dictates that they should be clipped to create a regular 4 foot gap between them. A *tapis vert* runs the length of the alley, appearing to reflect the strip of sky above. In spring the beauty of this effect is heightened by crocuses, snowdrops and violets.

The villa lies at the far end of the alley overlooking a small parterre garden. Steps lead up from this level to the oval lemon garden above. The circular pool that once stood among the lemon trees has been converted into a swimming

pool, however the tritons and sea-creatures at its centre appear undisturbed by the change. The old *limonaie* that overlook the garden have been changed into covered terraces, used for al fresco tastings of the Rizzardi's famous wines. Standing between them one can enjoy a magnificent view of the hills framed by the avenue. The secret garden lies on the slope behind the villa, and is not generally open to visitors. It is linked to the *piano nobile* by a bridge, currently a rather ugly metal affair. Terraces planted with green parterres ascend the slope, and a huge stalactite creates a cascade for the water which flows from the nyphaeum at the top.

The *giardino segreto* has rather lost its purpose now that it is overlooked by the new buildings on the other side of the road. It is the only place in the garden where neglect and the intrusion of the modern world combine to detract from the beauty of the original layout.

Previous page: *Villa Rizzardi: the 'Roman' ruin.*

Left: *Villa Rizzardi: the 'green theatre'.*

Villa Rizzardi	
Nearest major town:	Verona
Advance booking:	Groups yes, individuals no
Owner:	Contessa Loredan Rizzardi
Address:	Negrar
Location:	Negrar is approx. 18 km north west of Verona. Take the ss12 for Trento from Verona, turning off it after approx. 6 km at Parona. Negrar is signposted off this road. On entering Negrar turn right over the bridge, then immediately left, following road for approx. 1.6 km to the villa. A sign will lead you to the carpark for garden visitors. The custodian's house is in the yard where you should park.
Open:	Individuals should apply directly to the custodian – avoid lunchtime. Groups must make arrangements with the owner: Azienda Agricola dei Conti Guerrieri Rizzardi, 37011 Bardolino, Lago di Garda. Tel: 045 7210028.
Admission:	Free
Wheelchairs:	No
Refreshments:	No, but the Rizzardi wines may be tasted here prior to purchase.
Lavatories:	No

VILLA TRISSINO

TWO EIGHTEENTH-CENTURY GARDENS WITH MAGNIFICENT VIEWS

HISTORY

There are two Trissino villas on the hillside over-looking the Agno Valley. The upper villa is built on the site of the castle that was the stronghold of the powerful Trissino family during the Middle Ages. The lower villa was built during the eighteenth century by the Trissino Riale, another branch of the same family.

More is known about the upper villa than the lower. During the fifteenth century the Trissino's feudal properties were absorbed into the Venetian Republic, and their castle fell into disuse. In the fifteenth and sixteenth centuries alterations were made to the building, but it was not until 1722 that Francesco Muttoni was employed to replace it with a new villa and to lay out a garden around it. Muttoni received the Trissino commission in the wake of a visit to Rome, where he had been deeply influenced by the work of Borromini. In Muttoni's original drawings for the villa and garden, Borromini's style is certainly apparent. Had it been completed, the extraordinarily ambitious design would have turned the cliff on which the old castle was built into a series of terraces linked by passages, walks, ramps, tunnels and steps. In the 25 years before his death in 1748, Muttoni only managed to complete a fraction of the enormous task that he had set for himself. When he died Gerolamo dal Pozzo took his place, but much of the original plan was abandoned.

Little is known of the history of the unfortunate lower villa. It was built at about the same time as the other villa. At the beginning of the nineteenth century it passed out of the hands of the Trissino Riale and became the property of the Trissino Baston, who still owned the upper villa. In 1841 it was destroyed by fire, rebuilt, burnt down again some years later and then abandoned.

The two villas passed out of the Trissino family to the Da Porto family, and they now belong to the Marzotto family.

Villa Trissino: statues in the deserted lower garden.

Villa Trissino: Fountain of Neptune in the lower garden.

THE GARDEN

Perched on its crag above the Agno Valley, the upper villa at Trissino can be seen from many miles away. The task of transforming the sheer and rocky hillside into a garden could scarcely have been more challenging, and yet, if the difficulties of the site could be overcome, the magnificent setting ensured a startling result.

Muttoni's triple gateway acts as a flamboyant introduction to the garden. The ornate wrought-iron gates are crowned with an extraordinary mixture of scrolls, pinnacles, flaming torches and urns. The first gate was to lead to the terraces with which Muttoni planned to transform the hillside. It now creates a curious effect by opening onto thin air. The second gate leads to the lower terrace, and the third acts as an entrance to the triangular hanging garden.

The hanging garden is reached by a curiously complex route. A grotto containing a water-worn statue of Pan conceals the base of a curving ramp. The ramp leads up through a tunnel and emerges on a balustraded terrace overlooking the magnificent view. Rough grass and weeds now swamp the hanging garden, which was intended to be laid down to lawn. A minaret built onto the retaining wall encloses a spiral staircase. Sadly, it is too decrepit to be safe, but Muttoni's intention was that it should be used as an alternative route to the lower terrace.

Dal Pozzo is said to have had the ingenious idea of linking the hanging garden to the villa by means of a long balcony. The balcony runs around the *piano nobile* along the wall that encloses the secret garden and emerges on the belvedere.

The lower terrace is lined with pots of lemon trees and classical statues. It runs below the retaining wall of the hanging garden, and at its far end it opens out into a curious hexagonal garden. The trees on the slope below have grown to such a height that they now enclose the garden on two sides. This detracts from Muttoni's intention, which must surely have been to create a garden which seemed to hang in space above the breathtaking view. Scrolled stone seats are set into the angles of the hexagonal wall. The garden is laid out in a formal pattern of geometric beds divided by gravel paths. The beds are surrounded by raised stone borders, forming elaborate patterns which incorporate the Trissino family crest. These borders must be virtually unique, and it would be tragic if they were lost to the neglect that threatens to destroy them.

During the nineteenth century the Trissino turned the wooded area immediately behind the terrace into a memorial garden. Family monuments and tombstones stand among the trees, creating a fascinating and rather lugubrious effect.

One of the many paths that lead through the woods runs below the huge supporting structure of the hanging garden. The other retaining wall forms the boundary of the secret garden outside the villa. It is covered in roses and decorated with niches containing statues. Opposite the main entrance of the villa's new wing there is a sizeable grotto. When we were there it enshrined the wreck of a racing car. It was a disturbing discovery. We were relieved to hear that Count Marzotto, who is well known as a professional racing driver, had escaped alive from that particular accident.

A curving drive runs down through the woods from the end of the lower terrace to the villa below. The gardens of the two villas bear no relationship to each other, and the name of the lower garden's designer is not even known. At the beginning of the nineteenth century there was a plan to terrace the hillside, thus creating a link between the villas, but the death of the architect, Ottone Calderai, put an end to this.

The lower villa still stands, but it has no roof and the ground floor has been used to house animals. The windows of the main façade, which are now bricked up, once overlooked the wide terrace that runs below it. The balustrade is overgrown with Russian vine, and the grass that covers the steps to the lower garden is so long that we had to beat a path through it.

What was once a vast lawn below the terrace is now a mass of rough grass and flowering weeds. At its centre there is a large hexagonal pool. The effect of this simple layout is enormously spacious. It is overlooked on all sides by an infinite number of statues, which are attributed to Orazio Marinali and Giacomo Cassetti. They stand in a circle around the pool; they line the balustrades that form the boundary of the garden; they even look down from the upper terrace. The effect is of a vast and courtly ball, where the guests are an incongruous mixture of Venetians and ancient Romans. Most of the figures were produced in 1715, and the weather has been doing its worst since then. Many of them have lost limbs, all of them are covered in lichen, and some in Russian vine. It is almost impossible to read their names, which were once inscribed at the base of each pedestal.

On the far side of the pool the garden's rectangular form is broken by a semicircular terrace. Flights of steps lead down to what was once a lower walk, and is now a wilderness of nettles. Neptune looks out from the brambles beneath the retaining wall.

Villa Trissino	
Nearest major town:	Verona
Advance booking:	Yes
Owner:	Conte Giannino Marzotto
Address:	Piazza Trissino
Location:	Trissino is approx. 50 km north east of Verona. Take the A4, direction Padua, leaving it at the exit marked Montecchio. Go through Montecchio Maggiore on the ss246 for Valdagno. Trissino is approx. 11 km from Montecchio, and the villa is signposted up the hill from the town centre.
Open:	Strictly by prior arrangement: letter or telephone.
Admission:	Free
Wheelchairs:	No
Refreshments:	No
Lavatories:	No

TUSCANY (TOSCANA)

Tuscany runs from the central mountain ranges of Italy west to the coast. It contains a wide variety of landscape, from the Maremma marshes to the Apennine heights. The best known region is undoubtedly the rolling hills of the Chianti. The summers are hot, and the winters cold but short.

As the papacy has been to the history of Rome, so were the Medici to Tuscany. During the fifteenth century Cosimo de'Medici and his grandson Lorenzo (il Magnifico) made the city into the birthplace of the Renaissance. The Medici were subsequently expelled from Florence on several occasions, but always managed to return. In 1569 the Grand Duchy of Tuscany was created, with another Cosimo de'Medici as the first grand duke.

The Medici line became increasingly decadent and died out in 1743, when Tuscany passed to the House of Lorraine. From 1865 to 1871 Florence was the capital of Italy.

With a few exceptions, the typical early Tuscan garden tends towards the domestic in scale. A cypress avenue, a bowling alley, a few 'garden rooms' with simple parterres; visual magnificence may be provided by a grand view, according to Alberti's recommendations. The architectural grandeur of the Roman style was resisted in Tuscany throughout the Renaissance.

Palazzo Piccolomini: the view from the piano nobile.

VILLA ARRIGHETTI

CHARMING MODERN GARDEN IN THE TUSCAN STYLE

HISTORY

There has been a villa on this site since 1472. In 1602 it was bought by Giulio di Filippo Arrighetti, who rebuilt it in its existing form. A plaque on the façade commemorates the friendship between the Arrighetti and Galileo, who lived out his tragic old age in Arcetri, nearly blind and effectively under house arrest because of his contentious theories.

Little is known of the subsequent history of the villa. The garden was laid out during the 1950s, when the villa was bought by Anna d'Orleans. The villa is now run as an old people's home by an order of nuns.

THE GARDEN

Rather like the better known I Tatti, Arrighetti represents a foreigner's interpretation of the Tuscan garden. However, the designer has not attempted to recreate the style of a particular period, but has drawn on the traditional features that are to be found in the Tuscan gardens of every century. The result is one of considerable grace and harmony on a domestic scale.

The steep slope behind the villa has been transformed into a series of level terraces, each one enclosed by hedges or a low, undulating brick wall.

A shady terrace behind the villa overlooks the central portion of the garden. Parterres brimming with roses and brightly coloured annuals are set out around a lily pond. The beds are beautifully maintained by a single gardener. A flight of stone steps links the garden to the old *limonaia* above. Below the retaining wall of the terrace, a charming neo-classical statue, entwined with roses, stands in a shallow niche.

A cypress avenue flanks the grassy path leading down the slope below the garden. In summer, banks of purple irises grow beneath the trees. A centrally planted cypress provides a visual stop to the avenue. However, beyond the tree it curves round to open discreetly onto the main road below.

The Tuscan tradition of allowing the garden to merge with the surrounding countryside has been an inspiration to the designer of Arrighetti. The gravel paths leading away from the formal area give way to mown grass, and a long pergola of Russian vine leads into the heart of an adjacent olive grove.

Villa Arrighetti.

Villa Arrighetti	
Nearest major town:	Florence
Advance booking:	No
Owner:	Suore Stabilite nella Carità
Address:	Via della Torre del Gallo 8, Arcetri, Florence
Location:	South of Florence. Take the Viale Galileo Galilei west from the Piazzale Michelangiolo. Arcetri is signposted to the left shortly afterwards. The villa is on the right about 1 km up this road.
Open:	Ring the bell at the gate, morning or afternoon, no appointment necessary. Closed Sun
Admission:	Free
Wheelchairs:	Yes, as far as terrace overlooking upper garden.
Refreshments:	No
Lavatories:	No

GIARDINO DI BOBOLI

SIXTEENTH-CENTURY MEDICI GARDEN • CYPRESS AVENUE • ISLAND • EXCELLENT STATUARY

HISTORY

The Boboli gardens were for several centuries the private gardens of Palazzo Pitti, or the Pitti Palace, home of the illustrious Medici family. For the last hundred years they have served as the public gardens of Florence. Despite this they retain much of their former grandeur.

Palazzo Pitti, begun in 1453 to the design of Brunelleschi, is named after its original owner, Luca Pitti. He was one of the wealthiest men in Florence, and was used as a political pawn by the Medici throughout his life; they gave him 20,000 florins towards building costs in return for political services rendered. Ironically, in 1549, Eleanora, wife of Cosimo I, bought the palace from Luca's

descendants for a mere 9,000 florins. There are no records of any significant gardens prior to Eleanora's purchase.

Eleanora, who was considered to be of an *'insupportabile gravità'* (in other words an intolerable bore) by the people of Florence, also purchased the hillside behind the palace. The greater part of the land was owned by the Borgoli family, hence the similar-sounding name Boboli. The last Borgoli to farm the land apparently never recovered from parting with it. His is one of the very few attested ghosts in Italy – he is said to be seen about the gardens to this day.

In 1549 Niccolò Tribolo laid out the central

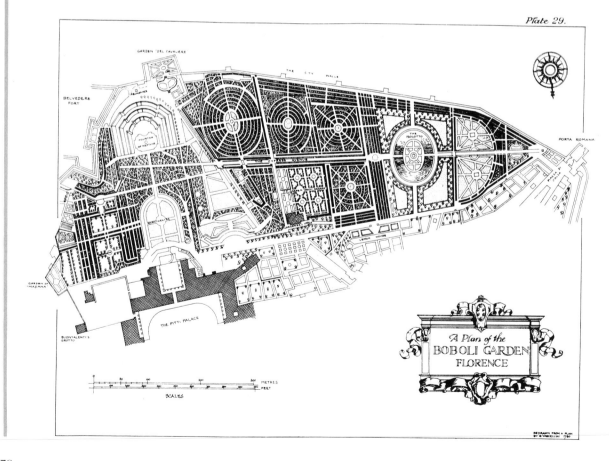

Plate 29.

A Plan of the
BOBOLI GARDEN
FLORENCE

axis of the garden, while continuing his work on another of Cosimo's gardens at Castello. He created the pool that lies above the palace, and the descent from it, which passes through the natural hollow that was later to become the amphitheatre. He died the following year, worn out, according to Masson, by the effort. The task of constructing the garden was taken up by Buontalenti, Ammanati and, later, the Parigi brothers.

In 1560 Cosimo and Eleanora moved to the Palazzo Pitti from the Palazzo Vecchio. Work on the building had not finished, but it is said that Eleanora could wait no longer to move into more spacious surroundings where she could accommodate her collection of rare plants and animals. Sadly, she died within two years of moving.

These gardens were rarely used as a place of individual refreshment or retreat. They have always been 'public' gardens in the sense that their principal function was the display of Medici wealth and power. It was to this end that a series of festivities were held during the sixteenth and seventeeth centuries. One of the most famous was the 'Naumachia' of 1589, performed as part of the elaborate marriage celebrations for Ferdinando I and Christine of Lorraine. The sunken courtyard behind the palace was flooded and eighteen Christian galleons were seen to besiege a Turkish castle. In 1631 the hollow behind the palace, whose potential Tribolo had largely ignored, was transformed into an amphitheatre with six tiers of stone seats. This provided an ideal setting for festivities on an even grander scale. The marriage of the future Cosimo III to Marguerite Louise d'Orleans was marked by a performance of *Il Mondo Festeggiante*. This was a combination of masque, pageant and equestrian ballet, in which Cosimo himself appeared as Hercules in jewel-studded armour. There were 20,000 spectators, but, unfortunately, the performance failed to impress the princess. Asked if she liked Florence, she replied that she would like it better if it were nearer Paris.

With the unification of Italy, the gardens passed to the State, and have been open to the public ever since. As a result of a recent conference there are major plans for restoration. The 200 garden statues (80 of which are Roman originals) are suffering increasingly from air pollution. There is a proposal to replace them all with replicas, and to display the originals in the converted palace stables.

THE GARDEN

On entering the garden from the palace you will find yourself in Buontalenti's grotto, built in 1583 and recently restored. It is the largest and most important grotto of the period, with three chambers richly decorated with shell and mosaic. It contains two lovely pieces of sculpture, Giambologna's 'Venus', and a copy of Michelangelo's 'Slaves' – the original is now in the Accademia. The grotto once contained *giochi d'acqua*, but these are now defunct. It was undergoing restoration at the time of writing, and closed to the public. Following the driveway round to the rear of the palazzo, you arrive in the great amphitheatre which lies on the main axis of the garden. Because of the sloping ground there is a sunken courtyard between the palazzo and the amphitheatre, containing Ammanati's Grotto of Moses. There is a large pool inside this, which, delightfully, has putti swimming in it. Several different fountains stood above the grotto before the present one was installed in 1641.

The amphitheatre, built in 1631, is a simple semicircle with six tiers of stone benches. It is extraordinary how little the Tuscan designers learned from their Roman counterparts (despite the existence of four Medici popes). This severe and ponderous design was created here while elsewhere in the country the baroque era was in full swing.

From the amphitheatre a double flight of steps leads up to Tribolo's pool and the Fountain of Neptune (1565) by Stoldo Lorenzi. This once stood above the Grotto of Moses. Higher still stands Giambologna's great statue of 'Abundance', erected to symbolise the benevolent rule of Ferdinando II de'Medici. It was originally made as a portrait of Joanna of Austria, wife of Francesco I, but her husband subsequently lost interest in both his wife and her statue. Below the walls of Fort Belvedere to the north is the *Kaffeehaus* of 1776. There is a small restaurant here with a fine view over the city.

Giardino di Boboli. The Art of Garden Design in Italy, *Triggs. 1906. (Bodleian. 19187 b.6.)*

Giardino di Boboli: the 'Isolotto'.

found this delightful baroque fantasy to be the most attractive feature of the gardens. It was laid out by Alfonso Parigi in 1618. The island is linked to the shore by bridges lined with lemon trees. The gates at the end of each bridge are crowned with goats, a reference to Cosimo III's astrological symbol. A copy of Giambologna's great statue of Oceanus stands in the centre of the island (the original may be seen in the Bargello). It is supported by figures representing the three greatest rivers known at that time, the Nile, the Ganges and the Euphrates. There is also a dramatic figure of Perseus riding through the water to the rescue of Andromeda, who is chained to her rock at the far end of the pool.

The line of the cypress avenue continues directly towards the Porta Romana exit. Or you can turn right towards the huge *limonaia*, which takes you back to the amphitheatre.

Giardino di Boboli	
Nearest major town:	Florence
Advance booking:	No
Owner:	The State
Address:	Palazzo Pitti, Firenze
Location:	Behind the Palazzo Pitti in central Florence. Entrance on left as you face the palazzo.
Open:	Daily Nov–Feb, 9–4.30 Mar–Apr, 9–5.30 May–Aug, 9–7.30 Sep–Oct, 9–5.30 Closed on national holidays
Admission:	Free
Wheelchairs:	Yes
Refreshments:	Yes
Lavatories:	Yes

Walking in the other direction you reach the splendid cypress avenue, which descends steeply through a labyrinth of paths and groves. It is lined with classical statues and was originally grassed over. The effect of the shaded, mossy descent, broken at intervals by shallow stone steps, must have been very beautiful. A few of the steps remain, but, sadly, the path was gravelled at the turn of the century. The groves on each side are what remain of the *ragnaie*. Also in this area were the maze and the botanical gardens, which have not survived.

At the foot of the avenue lies a large oval pool and lemon island, known as the 'Isolotto'. We

VILLA MEDICEA DI CASTELLO

SIXTEENTH-CENTURY MEDICI GARDEN

HISTORY

The villa was acquired by Lorenzo di Pierfrancesco de'Medici in 1477. On his death it passed to Giovanni delle Bande Nere, who was Grand Duke Cosimo I's father.

Cosimo became the first Grand Duke of Tuscany in 1537. The following year he decided to replace the existing layout at Castello with a new garden that would reflect the magnificence of the Medici. It is said that he asked Benedetto Varchi to plan it for him. Varchi was best known as a historian, and it seems likely that he was responsible for the iconography of the garden, while Niccolò Tribolo took practical responsibility for the realisation of his ideas.

In 1549 Tribolo accepted the additional task of designing the Boboli gardens for Cosimo. He died the following year, and his role at Castello was taken on by Buontalenti. Ammanati and Giambologna were both called upon to contribute sculptures.

Cosimo died in 1574; it is said that he spent the last years of his life at Castello in the company of his second wife Cammilla Martelli.

Vasari visited Castello in 1580 and described it as 'the most rich, magnificent and ornamental garden in Europe'. He also referred to a mulberry avenue flanked by canals that was to have run down the hill in front of the villa, linking it to the Arno. Sadly, this part of the grandiose plan was never realised.

At the end of the sixteenth century Castello was included in a series of lunettes by Utens. The structure of the garden is instantly recognisable, although the details are sadly changed.

Like so many of the early Tuscan villas, Castello was built next to the road. The forecourt, which was adorned with two oblong fishpools, served as a setting for games and tournaments. Sadly, the pools were filled in at the end of the eighteenth century, and the space is now used as a carpark.

Giardini segreti were laid out to either side of the villa. According to Vasari, the one to the west was planted with 'strange herbs'. These may have been the medicinal herbs that Cosimo imported from America. Montaigne visited Castello in 1580 and was delighted by a magnificent tree house in the garden to the east of the villa. Both of the *giardini segreti* were lost during the eighteenth century.

The main body of the garden has always been enclosed by high walls, making it resemble a medieval *hortus conclusus*. Vasari was delighted by the espaliered pomegranates and bitter oranges that grew against the wall, and the *berceaux* of scented cedar, cypress, olive and orange trees that shaded the paths.

Tribolo built two fountains. The first stood close to the villa, and was decorated with Ammanati's bronze of Hercules wrestling with Antaeus. The other was surmounted by Giambologna's statue of 'Florence' wringing water from her hair, and stood in the middle of a labyrinthine *bosco* of cypress, myrtle and laurel, which served to create a focus at the centre of the garden. Sadly, the fountain was moved to Petraia in 1760, the *bosco* was cut down, and the Hercules fountain was shifted to the centre of the garden. The eastern portion of the garden, which Tribolo had laid out as an enclosed orchard with a pavilion, was destroyed at the same time, and replaced by an area of 'English' woodland.

Castello was one of the first Italian gardens to be built around an iconographical theme. Every statue and fountain was designed to contribute to Varchi's complex programme, which mirrored the achievements of Cosimo I, and celebrated the establishment of the Medici as an absolute monarchy. Part of Varchi's plan was never realised, and its core was destroyed when the Florence Fountain was removed. However, it is still possible to piece together his scheme. The lower garden was to be seen as the lush and prosperous plain of Florence, presided over by Florence herself, who stood at its centre. Varchi originally intended that the little *bosco* should be peopled by statues representing the Medici virtues of Justice, Piety, Nobility, Valour and Generosity. Although this part of the scheme was never realised, the statue of Hercules struggling with Antaeus was to be read as the victory of Virtue over Vice. The water in which Florence bathes flows from the statue of Apennine on the upper terrace. It then descends through the wall fountains to either side of the grotto, which represent the Rivers Arno and Mugnone. Inside the grotto Cosimo is portrayed as the powerful unicorn, symbol of peace and purity.

Castello remained in the hands of the Medici until 1743, when the family died out and their property passed to the House of Lorraine. After the unification it became State property.

THE GARDEN

The gardens of Castello are laid out on a gentle slope behind the villa. The lower garden is completely enclosed by walls and flanked to the east by an area of 'English' woodland.

Castello merits a visit on account of its important history, its famous grotto and its magnificent collection of citrus trees. Visitors should, however, be prepared for the bleak prospect of the lower parterre garden. Tribolo's design has been destroyed by the loss of the little *bosco* that once stood at its centre. There are no longer any vertical features to relieve the monotony of the parterres. When we saw it, Tribolo's fountain had been stripped of Ammanati's bronze and was surmounted only by the ugly metal rod that supports it.

A low wall and a flight of shallow steps divide the parterres from the lemon garden. The Medici had always made a hobby of gardening, and like so many illustrious families they delighted in the collection and cultivation of citrus fruits. They were particularly interested in *bizzarie*, or 'bizarres', which they created by careful grafting. In this way they were able to produce multicoloured fruits, fruits with corrugated skins and others which resembled breasts, horns and buttocks. These strange objects were offered as precious gifts to visitors, and exchanged with other enthusiasts. Citrus flowers were sometimes dried and ground into a powder which was added to food as a seasoning and to wine as a kind of preservative.

Visitors can still see 600 different varieties of citrus trees at Castello. Some of the trees are 200 years old. Originally each pot was carefully labelled. Over the years, however, many of the labels have been lost, and even experts have found themselves unable to identify every plant. The magnificent collection narrowly escaped destruction during the unusually cold winter of 1985, when the plants were saved by the head gardener, who got up in the middle of the night to light fires in the *limonaia*.

Tribolo's famous grotto is at the centre of the retaining wall behind the lemon garden. Its roof is decorated with elaborate shellwork and tufa which takes the form of masks, Florentine lilies and arabesques. *Giochi d'acqua* are concealed in the mosaic floor, and pink and white marble basins encrusted with sea creatures adorn the walls. Water pours into the basins from the mouths and beaks of an extraordinary collection of animals and birds carved out of coloured marble. There are oxen and goats, a stag and a wild boar, a camel, a cat and an elephant, to name but a few. It is thought that this strange assembly was inspired by the tales of Renaissance travellers.

Two flights of steps lead up from the lemon garden to the upper terrace, where 'Appenino' stands shivering at the centre of his pool. The bearded face and naked torso of Ammanati's statue rise out of the long grass. Drops of water run in rivulets down his beard, giving the impression that Apennine is sobbing with cold.

Villa Medicea di Castello

Nearest major town:	Florence
Advance booking:	No
Owner:	State
Address:	Castello, Firenze
Location:	In the northern suburbs of Florence. From central Florence follow signs for Sesto Fiorentino until Castello is signposted to the right. The villa is signposted to the right shortly afterwards.
Open:	Nov–Feb, 9–4.30 Mar–Apr, 9–5.30 May–Oct, 9–6.30 Closed Mon
Admission:	Free
Wheelchairs:	Yes, with assistance
Refreshments:	No
Lavatories:	Yes

VILLA CETINALE

SEVENTEENTH-CENTURY GARDEN IN FINE HILLSIDE SETTING

HISTORY

It would be difficult to do better than to quote the words of Joseph Forsyth, an antiquarian traveller who visited Villa Chigi, as it then was, in about 1800.

> Cetinale which lies in a wide scraggy oak-wood about ten miles from Siena, owes its rise and celebrity to the remorse of an amorous cardinal who, to appease the ghost of a murdered rival, transformed a gloomy plantation of cypress into a penitential Thebais, and acted there all the austerities of an Egyptian hermit.

The 'amorous cardinal' was Flavio Chigi, Prince of Farnese, Duke of Ariccia and Prince of the Holy Roman Empire. He was the nephew of Pope Alexander VII and, it is said, the last cardinal to be appointed solely by virtue of a family relationship. He employed Carlo Fontana to plan the villa and gardens in 1680. He must have been an unusual man; Harold Acton quotes an inscription on the villa as follows: 'Whoever you are who approach, that which may seem horrible to you is pleasing to myself. If it appeals to you, remain. If it bores you, go away! Each is equally agreeable to me'.

After the cardinal's death the villa passed to his nephews, the Chigi-Zondadari. It remained in their possession until it was acquired by the present owner in 1977, in a very neglected condition. Since then it has been meticulously and beautifully restored.

Villa Cetinale: the villa and its surroundings seen from the hermitage.

THE GARDEN

Cetinale is enclosed by a great arm of mountainside, densely covered with oak woods. As at Il Bozzolo (see page 28), only a garden plan of the utmost simplicity could hold its own in so grand a setting. Fontana's plan could hardly have been simpler. Everything stands on a single axis which runs straight from the valley to the mountain skyline, a distance of nearly 3 miles.

The foot of the axis is marked by a great statue of Hercules standing among the woods. The line dips down to a stream, and then up towards the villa as a *tapis vert* between double rows of ilex. Passing through the gate, and receiving a noisy welcome from the household dogs, you enter the walled lemon garden in front of the villa. On the left are the *limonaia* and the family chapel. Statues by Mazzuoli decorate the central path. A shaded lime walk runs around the villa to the main entrance on the far side. Here a double flight of steps runs up to the *piano nobile* on the first floor. This is unusual for the area, but Fontana followed the Roman custom of reserving the ground floor as the domestic regions.

A broad grass avenue runs towards the ilex-covered hillside. It draws the eye upward to the focal point of the design, which is the hermitage placed far above on the skyline. This is thought to be the full extent of the original design. On the left of the *viale*, close to the villa, there is a sunken garden, laid out by the English wife of one of the Chigi at the turn of the century. The owners have restored the garden to its former beauty, planting old roses, scented climbers and large, informal colourful beds. It is a place to inspire a nostalgia for England.

The cypress avenue finishes at a pair of gates, now permanently open, ornamented with busts and two large figures by Mazzuoli. From this point an open grass walk continues to a raised terrace, where there is a gate into the woods beyond. Rough stone steps form a 'Scala Santa', ascending steeply to the hermitage.

The woods contain the 'Thebaid' referred to by Forsyth. A fairly common theme during the seventeenth century, the name derives from the communities of the Desert Fathers around Thebes in the first centuries AD. Paintings on the subject were often used to decorate rooms reserved for meditation and prayer. At Cetinale it takes the form of a number of forest walks lined with small chapels and statues of the disciples and other figures representing penitence.

It is worth making the climb to the hermitage, for the view is glorious. The building itself is much larger than it seems from the villa. Five storeys high, it has a central alcove containing a great cross of Lorraine the height of the building. Niches at each extremity of the cross hold busts of Christ and the four Evangelists. Sadly, the interior has been vandalised, but it is still possible to climb to the top and see Cetinale laid out below you, white doves circling over its roof and the olive groves spreading around it.

Villa Cetinale	
Nearest major town:	Siena
Advance booking:	Yes
Owner:	Lord Lambton
Address:	Cetinale, Sovicille, Siena
Location:	Cetinale is about 12 km west of Siena. From Siena take ss73 (Massa Marittima). After about 7 km turn right for Sovicille. 2 km further turn right for Ancaiano (unsurfaced road). On rejoining main road turn right and follow signs to Cetinale.
Open:	By appointment only (letter or telephone)
Admission:	Free
Wheelchairs:	No
Refreshments:	No
Lavatories:	No

VILLA DE'GORI

SEVENTEENTH-CENTURY GARDEN OVERLOOKING SIENA • ILEX TUNNELS • GREEN THEATRE • *RAGNAIA*

HISTORY

These gardens are known to have been laid out in 1620, when the villa was built for the de'Gori. It remained in the family until shortly before the last war, when it was bought by the Muratori. Signora Ginaneschi, née Muratori, still lives there today.

During the Second World War the villa fell victim to a bomb intended for the station below. Although everything else was destroyed, the garden and the villa's beautiful baroque façade miraculously escaped damage. The villa's historical importance was such that it was rebuilt behind the façade, in accordance with the original plans.

Villa de'Gori: the ilex avenue.

THE GARDEN

The seventeenth-century terraces that once lay in front of Villa de'Gori disappeared long ago. However, four of the garden's original features have survived, and they combine to create an interesting and unusual layout.

The villa stands at the junction of two long tunnels of gnarled ilex. One tunnel leads to the 'green theatre', and used to double as the entrance avenue. Over the centuries the roof of the tunnel grew lower and lower, until eventually it became imperative to create the new gateway that is used today.

The 'green theatre' is enclosed by a double ilex hedge, allowing the actors to move about backstage without being spotted by the audience. The wings are formed by a series of smaller cypress hedges, and a curved flight of shallow steps serves as seats for the audience. Turf and pebbles were used to form an elaborate pattern of beds between the seats and the stage. The turf has gone, but the slates that used to edge the beds remain to form a distinctive pattern. Although it is rather overgrown, the theatre would be a memorable setting for a performance of almost any kind. It was used most recently by the Ginaneschi children when they staged their own productions.

The second tunnel leads away from the villa at right angles to the first. Olive and fruit trees grow on either side of it, in what may once have been the terraced garden. The *ragnaia* lies at the far end of the tunnel. It consists of ilexes planted in a series of concentric circles and intersected by four slightly sunken stone paths. The *ragnaia*, or web, was concealed in a central clearing. It was made of netting smeared with bird lime. As if this wasn't bad enough, the decoy birds used to attract victims had to be blinded. This was said to make them sing, and a singing decoy is more effective than a silent one. Sadly, bird snares were a common feature in Italian gardens, providing both sport and sustenance. The one at Villa de'Gori is a particularly precious example, as very few have survived.

In front of the villa clipped cypresses form curious arches, and screen a glorious view of Siena. It is on account of these arches and its hillside position that the villa can be seen so easily from the city.

Villa de'Gori	
Nearest major town:	Siena
Advance booking:	Yes
Owner:	Avv. Giovanni Ginaneschi
Address:	Via Ventena 8, Siena
Location:	From Siena follow signs for Rome as far as the level crossing known as the Maddonina Rossa. Cross the line and go up the hill on Via dell'Osservanza. After approx. ½ km turn left, following signs for the Osservanza. Continue on this road for approx. ½ km, turning left onto Via del Paradiso. The road forks, Via Ventena is the left fork. The villa is to the right of the road – entrance at the far end.
Open:	Strictly by appointment – letter or telephone.
Admission:	Free
Wheelchairs:	Yes, with assistance
Refreshments:	No
Lavatories:	No

VILLA GAMBERAIA

PERFECT TUSCAN GARDEN • WATER PARTERRE • SUNKEN GARDEN • LOVELY RURAL SETTING

HISTORY

Villa Gamberaia derives its name from the first of a succession of owners. Matteo Gambarelli, for whom it was built at the beginning of the sixteenth century, was a stonemason. His sons Bernardo and Giovanni worked as architects under the name of Rossellino. Bernardo designed the Piccolomini Palace at Pienza.

At the beginning of the seventeenth century the property passed to Zenobi Lappi. In 1900 a broken shield was found in the garden, bearing the inscription: 'ZENOBUS LAPIT FUNDAVIT MDCX'. This probably means that Lappi virtually rebuilt the existing structure. When he died, in 1619, the property was inherited by his nephews, Jacopo and Andrea. Jacopo died in 1624. Andrea secured a good supply of water to the garden by purchasing various nearby springs and then buying the right to pipe the water over adjacent land. He is said to have developed a passion for building fountains. In 1636 he was taken to court by a neighbour after he had diverted the water supply from her villa. Sadly, there is no record of the garden that he created. It is hardly surprising, however,

that on Andrea's death, in 1688, the villa had to be mortgaged to pay off his debts.

In 1717 Gamberaia passed to the Capponi family, and under their care the garden assumed its present form. The architect's name is unknown and Zocchi's engraving, which was made at some point between 1735 and 1750, is the earliest record of the garden. At the end of the nineteenth century, Princess Ghyka of Serbia bought the villa and lived there with her American companion Miss Blood. It is to the princess that we owe the creation of the water parterre. According to the author Iris Origo, who grew up at Villa Medici in Fiesole, the princess was once a great beauty. As she grew older she took to wearing a veil and only left the villa to swim in the parterre pools at dawn, and to walk in the avenue after dark.

During the Second World War Gamberaia was virtually destroyed by bombs. Signor Marcello Marchi discovered it after the war and decided to restore the house and gardens to their original form. The garden has long been famous, and he was able to refer to numerous old prints, maps and

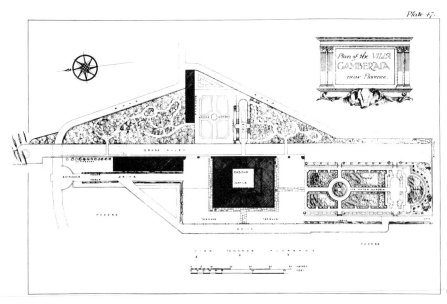

Villa Gamberaia. The Art of Garden Design in Italy. *Triggs, 1906. (Bodleian, 19187 b.6.)*

photographs for guidance. Signor Marchi still lives in the villa today.

THE GARDEN

For generations Villa Gamberaia has been cited as one of the most perfect examples of garden architecture. In an area of barely 3 acres it combines, in Edith Wharton's words: 'almost every typical excellence of the old Italian garden: free circulation of air about the house; abundance of water; variety of effect produced by the skilful use of different levels; and, finally, breadth and simplicity of composition'. The garden is beautifully maintained by three gardeners.

The gates swing open onto an imposing cypress avenue which serves to frame a small portion of

Villa Gamberaia	
Nearest major town:	Florence
Advance booking:	No
Owner:	Signor Marcello Marchi
Address:	Via del Rossellino 72, Settignano
Location:	Settignano lies beyond Fiesole, to the north east of Florence. Via Rossellino is beyond the main village piazza on the right. The villa is on the right after approx. 2 km. Parking outside the main gates.
Open:	Mon–Fri Winter 8–12, 1–5 Summer 8–12, 2–6
Admission:	L10000
Wheelchairs:	Yes
Refreshments:	No
Lavatories:	No

the villa. It is a simple rectangular building. The long east wall is extended at both ends by curious flying arcades. To the north, the arcade links the villa to the chapel, thus completing a continuous line of buildings that runs down to the gatehouse. To the south, a spiral staircase is concealed inside the arcade, linking the *piano nobile* to the parterre garden below.

The villa stands at the mid-point of the bowling green, which is one of Gamberaia's most beautiful features. The smooth lawn stretches the length of the garden, spanning a distance of about 200 yards. On one side it is flanked almost continuously by buildings, and on the other it is enclosed by the high retaining wall of the upper terraces. The wall is surmounted by urns and decorated with painted panels. In effect, the bowling alley resembles a quiet street, paved with grass and peopled by statues. At its northern end the perspective is closed by a nymphaeum standing in the shade of a group of ancient cypresses. Its walls are decorated with *spugne*, mosaics and bas-reliefs. The fountain inside is guarded by a satyr and two lions. At the other end of the alley a statue of Diana stands silhouetted against a magnificent view of the Arno Valley. The garden seems to extend beyond its boundaries into the olive groves and vineyards that surround it.

Opposite the villa the retaining wall is interrupted by a pair of wrought-iron gates decorated with the Florentine lily. These open into a sunken garden, which is enclosed on three sides by the retaining wall of the upper terraces. Bands of *spugne* and 'rustic' stonework divide the wall into panels. Smiling statues stand in the niches set into it. Four flights of balustraded steps link the garden to the lemon garden on one side and an area of *bosco* on the other.

The lemon garden is set out in front of the *limonaia*, and lies on a level with the *piano nobile* of the villa. Beyond it a path winds down through the trees to the end of the bowling alley.

The shady *bosco* on the other side of the sunken garden is planted with ilex and cypress and set about with statues and stone benches.

A loggia on the *piano nobile* of the villa's south façade overlooks the water parterre. This area of the garden has always been a parterre, and it is still laid out in the traditional manner around a central fountain. However, the roses and scented herbs

Villa Gamberaia.

that once filled the box-lined beds have been replaced by sheets of clear water. The effect of this imaginative transformation is quite delightful. Narrow paths run between the beautifully clipped hedges, and the composition is completed by a semicircular cypress arcade.

To the west, the villa overlooks a wide terrace bounded by a wall decorated with charming statues of dogs entwined with roses. Standing on the terrace you can enjoy the cool breeze and the scent of the roses while gazing at a magnificent view of Florence shimmering in the heat below.

VILLA GARZONI

BAROQUE GARDEN • GREEN THEATRE • WATER STAIRCASE • EXTRAVAGANT TOPIARY

HISTORY

The Garzoni family originated in Pescia, in the medieval Florentine Republic. Their political affiliations were such that they became exiles upon the death of Castruccio Castracani, the lord of Lucca, who led his troops to victory against the Florentines in 1325. The Garzoni sought refuge in Lucca, which soon became their home.

During the early years of the seventeenth century, the family bought the old castle of Collodi. It may be that they were attracted by its position on the border of the Republic of Lucca, overlooking their ancient home in the Grand Duchy of Tuscany. In 1652 they had the fortifications torn down to make way for a new villa.

While it was an ideal setting for a castle, the site posed many problems for the local architect entrusted with the work. The new building stood on the edge of a cliff, making it impossible to lay out a garden in front of it. To the rear, the space was occupied by the medieval houses of the village, which had once clustered around the castle walls. The architect, whose name is unknown, built the bridge to span the gorge to the east of the villa. In this way he linked the house to the steep slope beyond the gorge. The garden was then laid out both on the slope and also on the level ground below it.

When Ferdinand of Austria and Anna de'Medici visited Collodi in 1662, the villa looked much as it does today, although the garden was rather less striking in appearance.

It was not until 1786 that Ottavio Diodati, a local architect and man of letters, was employed to embellish the existing design. It is to him that we owe the terracotta statues, the *giochi d'acqua* and the 'green theatre'.

The villa belonged to the family until the beginning of this century. When the last Garzoni heir died, the property changed hands six times before it was bought, in 1945, by the late husband of the present owner, who restored and cherished the garden during his lifetime.

Villa Garzoni. The Art of Garden Design in Italy, *Triggs, 1906. (Bodleian, 19187 b.6.)*

THE GARDEN

A wooden door set into the high boundary wall serves as the visitors' entrance to the gardens. The villa itself is perched high on the cliff above. Before leaving the busy village street and entering the strange baroque world of the garden, you must wait for one of the six gardeners to answer to the ringing of the old brass bell.

The main body of the garden consists of a circular space enclosed by scalloped yew hedges. The considerable height of these hedges, and their strange undulating form, combine to create the impression that the garden is encircled by a vast coronet. A series of balustraded steps and terraces leads up to the base of the massive water staircase

Villa Garzoni.

that climbs the hill beyond. This striking and simple design is overlaid by a wealth of detail and colour.

The lower garden is a sort of menagerie: a peacock, a dinosaur and an elephant are among the topiary figures that stand about it. Real swans swim in Diodati's two circular fountains, and cages of exotic game birds stand in the shade of yew *berceaux*. These *berceaux* form a sheltered walk that runs around the perimeter of the garden. The swirling arabesques of *parterres de broderie* create the foreground of the lower garden. The simple rectangular parterres that lie beyond them are planted with brightly coloured annuals, arranged to form complex geometric patterns. On the gentle slope above, the plants give way to coloured pebbles, arranged to form the Garzoni.

The three sets of balustraded steps that lead out of the lower garden are another colourful sight. The retaining wall at each level is decorated with

mosaic. The balustrades and the strange little monkeys that adorn them are made of terracotta. Like all the terracotta figures in the garden, they were introduced by Diodati. Pots of trailing geranium stand between the monkeys on the balustrade.

Diodati installed *giochi d'acqua* in the grotto that is set into the retaining wall of the second flight of steps. Unsuspecting visitors were trapped by a wall of spray issuing from the step at the entrance. Additional jets sprang from the roof, the walls and the statue of Neptune. The victim could only avoid a soaking by standing perfectly still, and trusting that his host would soon tire of the sport.

The first terrace extends beyond the steps into an area known as the *Viale degli Imperatori*, named after the busts of Roman emperors that stand against the retaining wall. Diodati's 'green theatre' lies at one end of the terrace. It is completely enclosed by box and yew hedges. Gryphons holding *flambeaux* serve as footlights, and statues of Tragedy and Comedy stand to either side of the raked stage. There are charming terracotta shell seats in the auditorium.

The double water staircase climbs the rough hillside above the steps and terraces, cutting through the *bosco* on either side. It is the climax of the garden, and also serves to effect the transition from the cultivated to the wild, which was so important in baroque gardens. The staircase was originally fed by a spring that ran down the hill above the garden. Up to 400 barrels of water ran down the steps each hour, and went on to feed the pools below. This system has been replaced by a motorised pump, which draws water up from below. Unlike the spring, the pump does not always work, and some of the pools appear rather stagnant.

William Beckford, the English antiquarian and eccentric, visited Garzoni in 1780. His account provides us with a vivid image of the original force and effect of the water:

> . . . the sun broke from the clouds, and lighted up the green of the vegetation; at the same time spangling the waters which pour copiously down a succession of rocky terraces . . . The streams issue from a chasm in the cliff surrounded by cypresses, which conceal by their thick branches a pavilion with baths. Above rises a colossal statue of Fame, boldly carved, and in the very act of starting from the precipices. A narrow path leads up to the feet of the goddess, on which I reclined, whilst a vast column of water, arching over my head, fell without even wetting me with its spray, into the depths below.

The statue of Fame was another of Diodati's innovations. Originally two cypresses served to stop the eye at the head of the staircase.

The 'pavilion with baths' to which Beckford refers still stands at the head of the staircase, within easy reach of the villa. It has been closed to the public for several years, and we suspect that it is being allowed to fall into dereliction. There were once two magnificent marble baths, dressing rooms and salons. It is said that a small orchestra played in a screened gallery, and that screens between the baths allowed bathers to wash in private while continuing their conversation. As late as 1920, visitors described the sofas, which were still upholstered in their original faded silks, designed to match the white, blue and gold decoration of the walls.

Steep paths lead through the *bosco* to each side of the staircase. A dwarf, a Turk and a wild boar are among the terracotta figures that stand beneath the trees. Beyond the *bosco* a covered bridge spans the ravine and leads to the villa. It used to contain the controls for the *giochi d'acqua* that lie at the centre of the maze below. The bridge itself was also riddled with water jets.

The terrace in front of the villa affords a view across the garden to the surrounding countryside. Ducks and geese, kept to ward off snakes, live in the pavilions to either side of the terrace.

Villa Garzoni	
Nearest major town:	Lucca
Advance booking:	No
Owner:	Countess Grazini Gardi
Address:	Collodi
Location:	Collodi lies approx. 17 km north east of Lucca on the ss435 to Montecatini Terme. Collodi is signposted off the road 15 km from Lucca, and the villa is easily found in the centre of the village.
Open:	Nov-Apr, 8-1, 2.30-4.30; May-Oct, 8-dusk
Admission:	Garden only L7000; villa and garden L13000
Wheelchairs:	No
Refreshments:	Yes
Lavatories:	Yes

VILLA GEGGIANO

SIMPLE GARDEN IN RURAL SETTING • FINE EIGHTEENTH-CENTURY GREEN THEATRE

HISTORY

When the Bandinelli acquired Geggiano in the middle of the sixteenth century, it was a simple country villa with two medieval towers. It was not until 1780 that it was rebuilt in its present form. The loggia that was added to the first floor has since been closed, but in all other respects the villa is virtually unchanged, both inside and out. The walled garden and 'green theatre' date from the same period.

Alfieri, the famous Piedmontese playwright, spent a good deal of time at Geggiano. In 1783 the first edition of his tragedies was published in Siena. The plays were staged in the 'green theatre'.

During the Second World War the villa became a refuge for Ranuccio Bandinelli's friends, most of whom were painters, poets and writers, and many of whom were Jewish. In 1944 Bandinelli forestalled a German attempt to make a minefield out of the gardens by producing a letter from Kesselring, which he had actually removed from the front door of another building. The letter forbade the destruction of the villa on account of its historic importance. When he was cross-questioned, Bandinelli was quick to substitute Goethe's name for Alfieri's, and claim that it was one of his plays that had had its première there.

Left: *Villa Geggiano.*　　　Above: *Villa Geggiano: the kitchen garden.*

THE GARDEN

A curved avenue of cypresses marks the road to Geggiano. Beyond the avenue it is enclosed by hedges that have been clipped into an impressive variety of geometric shapes. The road then passes through a small *bosco* before arriving at one of the six ornamental gates that are set into the garden wall. Many of the stone and terracotta figures that decorate the wall have been broken, however the grimacing stone monkeys that stand above the lemon garden are a memorable sight.

The 'green theatre' lies opposite the villa. The raised stage is faced with bricks and dilapidated brick arches stand to either side of it. They were originally decorated with the crests of the Chigi-Zondadari and the Bianchi-Bandinelli, commemorating a marriage between these two families. A Maltese sculptor called Bosio executed the statues of Comedy and Tragedy that stand in the niches. The stage is enclosed by a cypress hedge, which made it possible for the actors to move around behind the scenes without being spotted by the audience. Clipped laurel forms the wings, and a single cypress creates a focus for the backdrop.

The lemon garden creates a delightful contrast to the somewhat dilapidated air of the theatre and its surroundings. The lemon trees stand to each side of a gravel path. The well-tended beds of vegetables and flowers that lie beyond them must be the pride and joy of the single gardener employed to tend the grounds. At the far end of the garden there is an enormous semicircular cistern.

Villa Geggiano	
Nearest major town:	Siena
Advance booking:	Yes
Owner:	Bianchi-Bandinelli
Address:	Pianella
Location:	Geggiano is approx. 8 km north east of Siena. Follow the ss408 from Siena for approx. 5 km. After Ponte al Bozzone turn left, following the sign for Villa Geggiano. The unsurfaced road continues for approx. 1½ km, before becoming the entrance avenue to the villa.
Open:	Strictly by prior appointment – letter or telephone. English spoken when the family is in residence, otherwise arrangements to be made with the gardener.
Admission:	Free
Wheelchairs:	Yes
Refreshments:	No
Lavatories:	No

VILLA GIULLARINE

TWENTIETH-CENTURY TRADITIONAL TUSCAN GARDEN •
VIEWS OVER FLORENCE

HISTORY

The name of the villa is derived from the Italian word for 'jester'. The village of Pian de'Giullari was originally the headquarters of the Florentine Guild of Jesters, who gave performances in a theatre in one of the villas. Villa Giullarine was built in the fifteenth century for the Bartolomeo family, but has changed hands many times since then. At the turn of the century it was bought by a Miss Daws, an American, who planted the cypress avenue and later erected the brick wisteria pergola. In 1938 it was bought by the present owner and her husband, who have devoted their lives to creating the lovely garden which can be seen today.

THE GARDEN

Despite its recent history, this garden is richly traditional. It is at one with the surrounding olive groves, and the imposing views over Florence sit easily with its friendly domestic scale. Far from having a neat symmetrical plan, it sprawls across the hillside so that you are inevitably drawn out into the countryside as you explore its paths.

An L-shaped walled garden borders the villa, providing an airy extension of the rooms on the ground floor. One arm contains the lemon garden with a nymphaeum, decorated in mosaic, at the far end. Flowerbeds to either side of the central path fill the garden with colour and scent. The outer garden wall is decorated with urns and busts.

Steps lead up from this garden to a small terrace on a level with the *piano nobile* of the villa. A screen of ilex has been planted along the edge. Box hedges clipped into scrolls surround a graceful fountain. The owners have indulged their humour here by training a wisteria in the shape of an umbrella over a circular stone table. Between the ilexes you catch glimpses of the distant horizon.

The greater part of the garden is roughly triangular in shape, with the sides formed by two pergolas and a cypress avenue. A third pergola, continuing the line of the avenue, extends the garden into the countryside. This entirely Tuscan mingling of artificial and rural landscape has been carried still further by the planting of an olive grove actually inside the garden. Below the avenue, outside the garden, the terraced famland is bright with flowers beneath the grey olive trees. By midday the air is sweet with the scent of rosemary, drawn out by the heat of the sun from the hedge along one side.

The avenue is bordered with irises and runs across the slope to a gate. Beyond, a wisteria pergola continues for nearly 100 yards. One side of it is closed by the boundary wall, while the other is open to the wonderful view and the olive groves that slope away down the hill. Back at the gate, another pergola leads up the slope to your right. A small statue at the top marks the apex of the garden. Returning down the third side of the triangle, you arrive on a balustraded brick terrace overlooking the olive grove at the heart of the garden. Cool arbours at either end are densely shaded by wisterias of great age, whose knotted stems threaten soon to uproot the balustrade. Two large olive trees seem to have made their way from the grove to the centre of the terrace.

The path continues to descend, shaded by trees and pergolas, until it reaches the *limonaia*. From this side of the garden there is a fine view over Florence, with the Duomo rising in the centre and the Apennines beyond. To the left there is a small terraced flower garden with double hedges of box and rosemary. Passing through an arch in a tall cypress hedge, you find yourself back on the terrace above the villa.

Villa Giullarine: the upper terrace.

Villa Giullarine	
Nearest major town:	Florence
Advance booking:	Yes
Owner:	Signora Gualino
Address:	Via del Pian dei Giullari 8/10, Arcetri, Firenze
Location:	South of Florence. Take the Viale Galileo Galilei west from Piazzale Michelangiolo. Arcetri is signposted to the left shortly afterwards. Follow this road for about 1 km. Take a sharp right turn into Via del Pian dei Giullari. The villa is about 180 m on the left. The road is very narrow and parking will be extremely difficult. Bus no. 38 runs to Arcetri from the railway station.
Open:	By prior appointment. Write or telephone to the caretaker (*custode*) at the villa.
Admission:	Free
Wheelchairs:	No
Refreshments:	No
Lavatories:	No

HORTI LEONINI
SIXTEENTH-CENTURY PUBLIC GARDENS

HISTORY

It is said that Cosimo I de'Medici awarded the site of the ruined citadel of San Quirico to the governor of the town to commemorate the cessation of hostilities between Florence and Siena. The governor was a loyal Medici supporter named Diomede Leoni. In 1581 the Governor of Siena wrote to Francesco I de'Medici, describing how Diomede was transforming the site into a walled garden, and had already restored the fortifications at his own considerable expense. It was already known as the 'Horti Leonini'; as with the Roman 'Horti Farnesiani' the use of *'hortus'* in the name is an indication of its importance.

The garden has always been public. It is thought that it was intended for the use of the many pilgrims who used to pass along the road to Rome. This is suggested by the various wall-plaques, with inscriptions such as: 'Surprise yourself with the splendour, smoke and noise of Rome' and 'Exhausted by the effort of pilgrimage we have returned to our own hearths'.

A tall medieval tower orignally stood in the upper garden. For centuries the symbol and the pride of San Quirico, it was destroyed by German troops in 1944.

The garden was later owned by the Chigi-Zondadari. It now belongs to the Comune.

THE GARDEN

The garden is divided into two sections by a *bosco* of ilex. Only the lower garden survives intact, and it is not known what form the upper garden once had. You enter from the piazza, under an arch formed by two ancient ilexes. The garden plan is one of simple but perfect geometry. Immaculately clipped double box hedges, in the form of a star, cover the whole area. In the centre there is a statue of Cosimo III de'Medici (by Giuseppe Mazzuoli, 1688). This is a recent addition, having been brought here from the Chigi palazzo in San Quirico in 1951. There is a small bed of roses. This is, however, predominantly a green garden, and its perfect symmetry and unity of colour make it an unusually tranquil place to spend time in.

Steps lead from the lower garden up through the *bosco*. The upper garden is now rough grass surrounded by ilexes, but there is a fine view of the Val d'Orcia from the surrounding walls.

Horti Leonini: the lower garden.

Horti Leonini	
Nearest major town:	Siena
Advance booking:	No
Owner:	Comune di San Quirico
Address:	San Quirico d'Orcia lies 40 km south east of Siena on ss2, the old road to Rome. The gardens are easily found in the centre of the town.
Open:	Daily, 8-dusk
Admission:	Free
Wheelchairs:	No
Refreshments:	No
Lavatories:	No

VILLA REALE

FINE SEVENTEENTH-CENTURY GARDEN ROOMS •
GREEN THEATRE • WATER THEATRE

HISTORY

The Villa Reale takes its name from the royal connections of two of its nineteenth-century owners. Since the fourteenth century the land had belonged to the Orsetti family. During the sixteenth century their defensive fortress was demolished, and a villa erected in its place. The gardens were laid out in the following century. The designer is not known.

In 1805 Napoleon crowned himself King of Italy. The following year he created his sister Elise Bonaparte Princess of Lucca and Piombino. On her elevation she compelled the Orsetti to sell their ancient home and set about transforming it into a Ruritanian court-in-miniature. Her husband Count Felice Bacciocchi became Minister of War and commander of the tiny Luccan army. Paganini was appointed as the royal director of music. Elise immediately set to work on the property, expropriating so much land from her neighbours that it doubled in size. The lovely Grotto of Pan, previously in somebody else's garden, was included at this time. The neoclassical gatehouses were also added during this period.

In 1811 she started to transform the garden, turning much of it into an 'English' park, and adding a huge ornamental lake. The seventeenth-century garden 'rooms' were probably saved by Napoleon's downfall in 1814. Elise was evicted, and the villa passed to its next resident. This was the erstwhile Duchess of Parma, the Bourbon Maria Luisa. She received the Duchy of Lucca in compensation for losing Parma, by a decision of the Congress of Vienna. They had decided to give the Duchy of Parma to Napoleon's wife Marie-Louise (daughter of the Austrian Emperor). Maria Luisa was succeeded by her son, who, in 1847, ceded the duchy of Lucca to Tuscany.

Villa Reale was later given to the widow of the Prince of Capua, whose family owned it until 1923. It was then bought by Count and Countess Pecci-Blunt, who restored it and added a small modern garden. It is still owned by their family.

Villa Reale: the Grotto of Pan.

THE GARDEN

The seventeenth-century garden is reached by crossing the broad *manège* that sweeps down from the villa to the lake. Statues are set into the banks of rhododendrons on either side. Although it looks as though it had been cleared during the nineteenth-century alterations, the *manège* is, in fact, an entirely traditional feature, and is recorded in the earliest engravings of this garden. On the far side, a short alley through the ilex woods leads to a gate into the lemon garden, This is the first in a series of garden 'rooms', which are made to feel successively more enclosed. At the northern end of this 'room' is a rectangular balustraded pool. It is overlooked by two bearded river gods (Arno and Serchio) and a nymphaeum containing Leda and the Swan. Real swans swim on the pool, disturbing the reflections of the lemon trees that line the balustrade. The nymphaeum is mirrored by an apse at the far end of the garden.

To the east of the pool, wrought-iron gates between heavily rusticated columns open into a circular 'anteroom'. Steps lead up to a smaller circular pool from which rises a single tall plume of water, brilliant against the background of dark yew and magnolia. The figures of the four seasons stand around the anteroom. Beyond, visible through the spray, is the 'green theatre'. It is perhaps the finest, although not the largest, in Italy. It is enclosed by 20 foot high yew hedges, with windows and doors cut into them. Footlights, orchestra pit, prompter's box and seating are all cut from box or yew. Lifesize terracotta *commedia dell'arte* figures stand in niches cut into the backdrop. The four gardeners clip all this, and the rest of the garden, by hand. It takes them nearly three months each year.

There is a simple 'water theatre' behind the villa. It consists of a semicircular pool filled from lion masks set around the wall behind it. A path runs around the top of the wall, backed by a high ilex hedge. The centrepiece is a grotto above the path, containing a stepped cascade.

South of the lemon garden you can find the sixteenth-century Grotto of Pan. This is an unusual two-storey structure lying deep in the woods. The exterior is entirely covered with mosaic and *spugne*. The open ground-floor loggia has a marble bowl in the centre, filled with trailing geraniums. The ceiling is decorated with stone plants and flowers, and has a star in the centre from which water can spray. Terracotta urns overflowing with *spugne* stand in niches. The grotto has a domed ceiling and a mosaic floor, with figures of Pan and accompanying tritons set in niches. On close inspection you can see the jets set around the walls, for what must have been a deluge of spray.

Villa Reale	
Nearest major town:	Lucca
Advance booking:	No
Owner:	Conti Pecci-Blunt
Address:	Marlia, Lucca
Location:	Marlia is 10 km north east of Lucca. Take the ss435 for Montecatini Terme. After 7 km turn left for Marlia and follow signs for Villa Reale. At traffic lights turn right following small sign to Ville Lucchese. Turn left at war memorial and follow garden wall to main entrance.
Open:	Daily – closed Mon Guided tours only: Summer 10, 11, 4, 5, 6. Winter 10, 11, 2, 3, 4. Aug, Sep: only open Tue, Thur, Sun
Admission:	L3000
Wheelchairs:	No
Refreshments:	No
Lavatories:	No

VILLA MEDICI

FIFTEENTH-CENTURY MEDICI GARDEN • MAGNIFICENT VIEWS

HISTORY

Cosimo the Elder bought the villa, which was known as Belcanto, from the Bardi in 1458. He employed Michelozzo Michelozzi to rebuild it, with the intention of giving the new house to Giovanni, his only son. The construction process was arduous and expensive, as foundations had to be sunk into the precipitous hillside. When the building was finished Michelozzo went on to lay out gardens around it, just as he had done at Cosimo's villas in Cafaggiolo and Careggi. It is said that Cosimo was doubtful about the charm of the new garden. He took no pleasure in the magnificent view, preferring his own country retreat at Cafaggiolo, where everything he could see from the windows belonged to him.

The villa and its garden were complete by 1461. Two years later Giovanni, who was immensely fat, died of a heart attack and Cosimo took no further interest in the place.

Villa Medici found favour again under Lorenzo il Magnifico, who took Cosimo's place as a leader among the humanists of the day, and as a member of the Platonist Academy. He was delighted by the garden, which he saw as a perfect setting for learned discussions, poetry readings and private meditation.

It is said that the members of the Pazzi conspiracy originally planned to murder Lorenzo and Giuliano at a banquet that was to be given at the villa. This proved to be one of numerous false starts. The banquet was cancelled when Giuliano injured his leg in a hunting accident, and the murderers finally resorted to attacking the brothers during High Mass in the Duomo.

In 1671 Cosimo III sold Villa Medici to Vincenzo di Cosimo Serra. This marked the beginning of a series of different ownerships. In 1772 it was bought by the Duchess of Orford, Robert Walpole's eccentric widow. The villa was almost completely rebuilt by the Buoninsegni family, who bought it in 1780. During the nineteenth century it became known as Villa Spence, having been bought by William Blundell Spence, the English painter and collector. In 1911 Lady Sybil Cutting bought the property and restored the lower garden with the help of Cecil Pinsent. Her daughter Iris Origo grew up there, and has written about her childhood at Villa Medici in her autobiography *Images and Shadows*.

THE GARDEN

Despite the virtual rebuilding of the villa during the eighteenth century, Michelozzo's garden escaped radical transformation. It is quite unlike the simple, almost medieval gardens that he designed for Cosimo's villas at Careggi and Cafaggiolo. Here, the precipitous hillside was cut into terraces which were set out to embrace the magnificent view beyond. Despite this radical departure from the tradition of the enclosed garden, Michelozzo did not consider it necessary to link the different levels of his design. Had he been working a hundred years later, he would no doubt have built ramps or steps between the terraces. As it is, the

Above: *Villa Medici.*

Right: *Villa Medici: the loggia.*

lower terrace can only be reached by a circuitous path that runs down from the entrance to the upper garden.

The upper garden seems to hang in space above the view, which stretches right across the valley below. The only boundary is a low brick wall, decorated with terracotta pots of red geraniums. On the other side the terrace is completely screened from the road by a high wall, which is said to be Etruscan in origin. To the east it is enclosed by the delicately frescoed loggia of the villa, and to the west by an elaborately decorated wall.

Much of the terrace is occupied by lawns, which are divided by paths and shaded by ancient paulownias. The paths are lined with pots of lemon trees, which are transferred to the *limonaia* in the corner of the garden each autumn. The narrow terrace that lies against the boundary wall is thought to date from the eighteenth century. It is planted with climbing roses grown in swags or festoons in the French manner.

The pretty nymphaeum at the far end of the garden is decorated with *spugne* and an elaborate pebble mosaic. The mosaic, which is made up of red, black, white and cream-coloured pebbles, extends onto the wall that flanks the main entrance.

On the other side of the entrance there is a beautiful seventeenth-century loggia. It is open on one side to the garden and on the other to the magnificent view across the valley. The back wall is decorated with a *trompe-l'oeil* painting of the garden. The same mosaic of shells, pebbles and *spugne* adorns the outer walls. At the back, the initials 'VS', for Vincenzo Serra, are set into the mosaic.

The ilexes that grow above the main drive have leant right over, creating a kind of tunnel. Steps lead up through the trees to a second terrace which lies above the *limonaia*. This part of the garden has been virtually abandoned. An overgrown cypress avenue extends beyond the remains of an elaborate grotto set into the side of the hill.

The lower garden was completely redesigned by Cecil Pinsent in 1911, although the magnificent raised pergola that runs along the bottom of the retaining wall may have been a part of the original layout. There is a similar pergola at Cosimo's villa in Cafaggiolo. Ancient wisteria entwines the balustrades of the steps that lead down from the centre of the pergola. Pinsent bowed to the splendour of the setting by creating the simplest of designs. Lawns, parterres and pots of lemon trees are arranged around a circular fountain. Like the rest of the garden, the lower terrace is meticulously maintained by a single gardener.

The last of Michelozzo's terrace gardens lies on the other side of the villa. It can be reached by walking to the end of the pergola and crossing the enclosed area below the building. Every detail of Michelozzo's original design has survived in this secluded hanging garden. Green parterres divided by gravel paths are arranged around a circular fountain. The shady stone seats set into the wall of the villa may once have been used by Lorenzo and his friends from the Platonist Academy.

Villa Medici	
Nearest major town:	Florence
Advance booking:	No
Owner:	Signora Anna Mazzini
Address:	Via Vecchia Fiesolana, Fiesole
Location:	Via Vecchia Fiesolana is a steep hill running west out of the central piazza in Fiesole. The villa is on the left at the end of a long wall. Ring the bell on the tiny door set into the wall of the villa. (NB: the door is painted the same colour as the wall, and is easily missed.)
Open:	Mon-Fri, mornings only
Admission:	L10,000 (for cancer research)
Wheelchairs:	No
Refreshments:	No
Lavatories:	No

VILLA DELLA PETRAIA

SIXTEENTH-CENTURY MEDICI VILLA

HISTORY

The land originally belonged to the Palla di Noferi degli Strozzi, whose fortress had stood there since the early fourteenth century. In 1427 it was confiscated by Cosimo de'Medici the Elder, and sold to the Salutati family. In 1568 Cosimo I de'Medici bought it back to give to his second son Ferdinando, who, having been made a cardinal at the age of fifteen, was living in the Villa Medici in Rome. In 1589 Ferdinando became grand duke following the death of his elder brother. He immediately commissioned Buontalenti to build him a villa at Petraia and to lay out gardens around it. The work was completed by 1595. The villa was built on the foundations of the ancient castle but retained its tall keep, which you can still see today.

The design of the garden has not remained unchanged. It is fortunate that it was recorded in a painting by Utens in 1599. It is the lowest of its three terraces that has changed out of all recognition. Buontalenti chose to lay it out with *berceaux* forming two large ovals. In the centre of each oval was another *berceau* in the form of a circle, containing a simple fountain. Paths intersected in the middle of each circle, forming an elegantly symmetrical plan. The spaces inside each oval were planted with fruit trees.

As early as 1609, the year of Ferdinand's death, there is a note referring to work being undertaken at Petraia 'in order to divide it up in the French

Villa della Petraia.

manner'. At least some of this work was carried out by Giulio Parigi, who added the central fountain on the lower terrace. In 1760 the Fountain of Venus was brought from Castello and installed on the upper terrace.

In 1865 Florence became the temporary capital of Italy, and Petraia was made into one of the royal residences. Vittorio Emanuele II and his second wife Countess Mirafiori spent much time here, often dining on a platform set into an ancient ilex on the upper terrace. Flowerbeds were laid out everywhere to suit the nineteenth-century taste, thus removing the last traces of the original planting.

THE GARDEN

We advise you to ignore the tempting lower entrance to the garden, and to make your way up the steep cobbled lane that leads to the villa. From the dark cypress woods that cover the hill above, a stream flows over a moss-covered cascade into a pool. This is situated opposite the façade of the villa. A door in the wall to the right leads into the lemon garden on the upper terrace. The centrepiece is formed by Tribolo's fountain, decorated with Giambologna's statue representing Florence, brought here during the eighteenth century (see page 81).

This terrace once commanded a fine view of the valley of the Arno with Florence and the surrounding hills. It is now sadly marred by industrial development, and the air is hazy with pollution. However, from the south-east corner of the lemon garden, where there is a small nineteenth-century loggia, there is still a good view of the city framed by trees. Here you can see how villa and garden were situated in accordance with Alberti's ideals, overlooking 'the city . . . or a great plain and familiar hills and mountains'.

Immediately below the upper terrace there is a long *peschiera* running parallel to the front of the villa. It is reached by a flight of flower-lined steps at each end. Jets of water are set along its length and the edge is lined with pots of trailing geraniums.

A central flight of steps leads down to the third and lowest level. This slopes down to a row of poplars, which lines the southern boundary of the garden. It is covered with a pattern of geometrical parterres filled with flowers. In the centre stands a

graceful fountain, surrounded by stone benches and a circular box hedge. To left and right of the fountain are *boschetti* of ilex, probably planted during the seventeenth century to replace Buontalenti's *berceaux*. The exit lies to the right, through the trees. It passes an area of rough grass which, when we were there, was filled with poppies, blazing against a background of black ilex bark.

Villa della Petraia	
Nearest major town:	Florence
Advance booking:	No
Owner:	The State
Address:	Castello, Firenze
Location:	In the northern suburbs of Florence. From central Florence follow signs for Sesto Fiorentino until Castello is signposted to the right. The villa is signposted to the right shortly afterwards. Also bus no. 28 from the railway station.
Open:	Daily Nov-Feb, 9-4.30 Mar-Apr, 9-5.30 May-Oct, 9-6.30 Closed Mon and national holidays Villa open daily 9-1.30
Admission:	Free
Wheelchairs:	No
Refreshments:	No
Lavatories:	Yes

PALAZZO PICCOLOMINI

FIFTEENTH-CENTURY HANGING GARDEN • LOVELY VIEWS

HISTORY

This small but spectacular garden is one of the earliest to have survived almost unchanged since its creation. In 1458 Aeneas Silvius Piccolomini was elected to the papacy as Pius II. Shortly afterwards he conceived the ambitious plan of rebuilding, as an ideal town, the village where he was born, Corsignano. It was to be renamed Pienza after himself. He turned first to Alberti, whose humanist ideals were close to his own. Alberti was not, however, a practical architect, although he was a distinguished architectural theorist. He suggested Bernardo Rossellino, who had recently completed Palazzo Rucellai in Florence, following Alberti's theories. He had also worked at the Vatican for Nicholas V.

Rossellino's brief was to draw up plans for the town and to be responsible for the building of the duomo and the palazzo, which stand next to each other in the central piazza. He quoted 18,000 ducats for the project. The site was difficult, being

Palazzo Piccolomini.

little more than 5000 sq. yards on the edge of a cliff. The ground was poor and foundations had to be dug to a depth of over 100 feet. Several of the workmen are still there, buried when the hole collapsed. To add to Rossellino's problems, as a Florentine he was held in contempt by the Sienese workforce.

By the completion of the work the cost had risen to over 50,000 ducats. A law of the time (one that might usefully be revived) required that Rossellino should repay the difference. Pope Pius, however, congratulated him and awarded him a cloak of honour, saying that if Rossellino had initially quoted him the true cost, the money would never have been raised and Italy would have been deprived of these marvellous buildings.

The palazzo remained in the possession of the Piccolomini until the death of the last member of the family in 1978. Since then the property has been administered by a charitable trust.

THE GARDEN

Despite the problems of construction, Rossellino treated the spectacular site with an impressive boldness. Palazzo Piccolomini is built on the edge of a high bluff, overlooking the whole of the Val d'Orcia. The garden lies in the tiny space between the palazzo and the edge of the cliff. On entering the square courtyard of the palazzo, you find the stairs to the *piano nobile* on your right. Immediately opposite is the garden entrance.

Having made a tour of the palazzo, you will see the garden first from the loggia on the *piano nobile*. The view is quite breathtaking. It is unchanged since Pius II wrote about it over 500 years ago:

> You look down into the valley of the Val d'Orcia, green fields and little hills covered with the season's growth, fields cultivated with fruit and vines, towns and castles and rocky precipices . . . and Radicofani, gateway of the winter's sun.

The garden lies at your feet. It is, in effect, a small garden 'room', with four rectangular parterres and raised beds around the walls. On the edge of the cliff a wall provides shelter. It is pierced with three arches so that you may, with one step, turn from the enclosed privacy of the garden to look out over the miles of open country-side below. Both palazzo and garden are designed specifically for the enjoyment of the view, obeying the humanist injunction that the surrounding landscape should determine the form of the garden. This is a radical shift from the inward-looking medieval desire to exclude nature in all but is domesticated forms.

Palazzo Piccolomini	
Nearest major town:	Siena
Advance booking:	No
Owner:	La Società Esecutori Pie Disposizioni, Siena
Address:	Pienza
Location:	Pienza is 50 km south east of Siena. From Siena take ss2 (the old road to Rome). After 40 km turn left at San Quirico. The palazzo is next to the cathedral in the centre of Pienza.
Open:	Daily 10-12.30, 3-6. Closed Mon. Entrance to the garden is on request after the tour of the palazzo. It is also seen from the loggia as part of the tour.
Admission:	L2000
Wheelchairs:	Yes in garden, but not in the palazzo
Refreshments:	No
Lavatories:	No

VILLA LA PIETRA

TWENTIETH-CENTURY ITALIANATE GARDEN • GREEN THEATRE • FINE STATUES

HISTORY

Villa La Pietra was originally built at the beginning of the fifteenth century for the Macinghi family. Its name, 'the stone', derives from the milestone which used to mark its distance from the walls of Florence. In 1460 it was bought by Francesco Sassetti, the leading Florentine banker under both Cosimo de'Medici and his grandson Lorenzo. After his death, in 1491, the villa was bought by the Capponi family. It owes its baroque exterior to Cardinal Luigi Capponi, who undertook substantial renovations during the seventeenth century. The work is thought to have been done by Carlo Fontana. The gatehouses were also added at this time.

The main garden was entirely destroyed when it was landscaped in the English manner during the nineteenth century. The smaller north garden survived and is now the lemon garden. The Capponi were also responsible for the garden at Villa Gamberaia (page 88), which may give a rough idea of how La Pietra was originally laid out.

In 1902 the villa was bought by Arthur and Hortense Acton, the parents of the present owner. Two years later they began to recreate an Italian garden on the site of the lost original garden. This enormous task was later continued by their son.

THE GARDEN

As at Villa Gamberaia, the entrance is by way of a dramatic cypress avenue, framing the house at the far end. Here, the avenue runs for nearly half a mile through the olive groves. The main garden is laid out on a series of broad terraces behind the house to the south east. The upper terrace has a stone balustrade ornamented with statues and busts. Steps lead down to the next level, with a central fountain surrounded by grass parterres. One of the purposes of the garden is the display of Arthur Acton's fine collection of statues. As you descend, intersecting paths continually draw your attention along them to cunningly placed figures at the far end. At the lowest level, an opening in a screen of yew reveals the Greek peristyle laid out around a central fountain. Classical statues stand between the Corinthian columns. To the left lies the 'green theatre' with its topiary footlights and wings, decorated with charming *commedia dell'arte* figures by Bonazza.

Many of the hedges are of immense height – 30

Villa La Pietra	
Nearest major town:	Florence
Advance booking:	Yes
Owner:	Sir Harold Acton
Address:	Via Bolognese 120, La Pietra, Firenze
Location:	Follow signs to the north for Bologna (ss65) from Piazza della Libertà. The entrance to the villa is on the right on a sharp bend 1½ km from the piazza.
Open:	From April to June with the Associazione Toscana Agriturist, Piazza San Firenze 3, Firenze, Tel: 055-287838
Admission:	L30,000 including two other villas, transport and refreshments
Wheelchairs:	No
Refreshments:	No
Lavatories:	No

feet or more – and the numerous garden 'rooms' give a strong sense of solitude and privacy. This is primarily an evergreen garden which does not depend on colour for effect. The play of sunlight and shade is cleverly used to give life to the deep greens of the enclosing hedges.

The walled lemon garden is to the north east of the villa. At the time of the Renaissance this was laid out with simple parterres. It is largely unchanged since Cardinal Capponi enlarged it in 1690 and built the *limonaia*, which is ornamented with *rocaille* work and has busts placed along the cornice. The walls surrounding the garden are similarly decorated.

La Pietra is a difficult garden to classify. Its conscious theatricality is the antithesis of the Tuscan style. Arthur Acton drew his ideas from many periods of garden design and from all parts of

Italy, but most of all from his own imagination. The result is the kind of Italian garden one might see in a dream, which is perhaps the answer.

Villa La Pietra.

VILLA CORSI SALVIATI

EIGHTEENTH-CENTURY GARDEN • GREEN THEATRE • MAZE

HISTORY

Villa Corsi Salviati has belonged to the family since the sixteenth century. Unlike the majority of its Tuscan counterparts, the garden occupies a level site. This may, in part, explain the extraordinary facility with which successive generations have changed it to conform with the fashions of the day.

When Simone di Jacopo Corsi bought the villa in 1502 it was a simple farmhouse. The garden that lay behind it consisted of a few patches of lawn arranged around a fountain. It was not until the beginning of the seventeenth century that three additional areas were added to the layout. The lawns were turned into grass parterres, and bounded to the east by a *bosco*. Beyond the trees there was a kitchen garden, enclosed on three sides by walls, and on the fourth by a *limonaia*. A bowling green stretched along the east wing of the villa. To the west, the parterres were bounded by a walled lemon garden. This was arranged around a circular pool which surrounded the rabbit island. A *ragnaia* was created beyond the southern boundary of the parterre garden. The villa itself was extended by the addition of a loggia, and a large aviary was built against the west wall.

In 1738 the villa was altered once again by Marchese Antonio Corsi, who responded to the fashion of the day by adding a graceful baroque façade. The two balustraded belvederes that sit to either side of the central block also date from this period. The aviary was transformed into an open loggia.

An engraving, executed by G. Zocchi in 1740, records the results of the marquis's work on the garden. The wall that divided the parterres from the lemon garden was taken down. The rabbit island was removed and the circular pool was incorporated into the central layout. Zocchi's print shows several jets of water rising from the surface of the pool, in imitation of the French fountains that had become so fashionable. Wrought-iron fences and ornate gates decorated with statues sur-

rounded the garden, just as they do today. The *ragnaia* which, like the lemon garden and the rabbit island, was too practical for the marquis's taste, was replaced by a short canal divided by little cascades. The *bosco* was extended into the area that had served as a kitchen garden.

During the nineteenth century the garden was altered yet again. The *bosco* was transformed into a romantic wood, with two mounds, a ruined 'castle' and a small lake with an island and a rustic hut. Palm trees were planted behind the villa, and two greenhouses were built to shelter Marquis Amerigo Corsi's rare and exotic plants, for which the garden soon became famous.

In 1907 Marchese Giulio Guicciardini-Corsi Salviati – the father of the present owners – set about restoring the eighteenth-century layout. Although the romantic woods were left largely intact, he pulled down the greenhouses and reinstated the parterres.

THE GARDEN

Looking at the parterre garden today, it is hard to believe that it dates only from the beginning of this century. The memory of the palm trees and exotics has been eradicated by the marquis's faithful reconstruction of the eighteenth-century layout.

The garden is enclosed on one side by the delightful façade of the villa. Woods lie to the west; to the south and east it is bounded by an ornate wall and a fence which is divided by pillars and adorned with numerous statues. Many of the statues are missing, but among those that remain are animals, classical figures, Tuscan peasants, urns and torches.

A simple fountain stands at the centre of the garden and around it statues and stone benches are arranged in a circle. The parterre beds, which are planted with brightly coloured annuals, form a series of small diamonds and rectangles. This was an arrangement that became popular in the eighteenth century. Pots of lemon trees stand among the parterres, adding to the colourful layout.

The oblong pool that lies to the west of the parterres also existed in the eighteenth century. Water flows into it from grotesque masks that decorate the walls. Statues of the four seasons mark each corner of the pool, which is enclosed by a balustrade decorated with terracotta pots of trailing geraniums. A loggia frescoed with classical ruins lies at the far end. It has taken the place of the seventeenth-century aviary.

A circular lilypond lies beyond the pool. This originally surrounded the rabbit island, and features in the foreground of Zocchi's print.

The eighteenth-century canal can still be seen cutting through the old *ragnaia* that lay opposite the villa, beyond the boundary of the parterre garden. It is made up of thirteen separate basins divided by little cascades. These were once decorated with water jets. The apparent length of the canal was increased by a fountain at its far end, which was decorated with a *trompe-l'oeil* created from *spugne* and mosaics. The wood to the east of the parterres is made up of ilexes, planted to create shady paths and groves. Very little is left of the statues that once stood among the trees. The romantic lake, spanned by a decorative bridge, is somewhat overgrown, as is the maze that the marquis planted on the site of the old greenhouses. Having no record of the seventeenth-century design, he drew his plans from the maze at Hampton Court.

A 'green theatre' lies below the east wing of the villa and in front of the *limonaia*. Although not a feature of the original layout, it was built during the restoration of the garden. One of the nineteenth-century mounds was used as a foundation, and its design was drawn from the plans of the theatre at Castle Mirabell in Salzburg. The narrow, mossy stage is enclosed by wings of clipped box. Apollo stands at the back of the stage on a pillar supported by turtles. The prompter's box is made from clipped box and enclosed by a dome of ivy.

A single gardener is employed to care for the grounds of Corsi Salviati. We were relieved to hear that he has part-time help during the pruning season.

Villa Corsi Salviati

Nearest major town:	Florence
Advance booking:	Groups yes, individuals no
Owner:	Conti Guicciardini-Corsi-Salviati
Address:	462 Via Gramsci, Sesto Fiorentino
Location:	Sesto Fiorentino is approx. 9 km north west of Florence. Via Gramsci is the main road into Sesto from Florence, and the villa is on the left just before you enter the town.
Open:	May-Oct, Tues and Fri 3-dusk
Admission:	Free
Wheelchairs:	Yes
Refreshments:	No
Lavatories:	Yes

Villa Corsi Salviati.

VILLA I TATTI

TWENTIETH-CENTURY TUSCAN GARDEN

HISTORY

I Tatti was built in 1563 as a simple farmhouse. It was later absorbed into the estate of La Vincigliata, the pseudo-medieval castle above Settignano. In 1905 Bernard Berenson, the famous American art critic and collector, bought the villa with 40 acres of land. Most of the land was planted with firs and cypresses, and the rough garden to the rear of the villa consisted of little more than a few fruit trees planted on a steep slope.

Since the eighteenth century there had been a large expatriate community of many nationalities in and around Florence. At the time that Berenson bought I Tatti, numerous other foreigners, many of them English, were buying villas in the hills surrounding the city. Some of the villas had been empty for years and their gardens had fallen into dereliction. Others had nineteenth-century *giardini all'inglese*. Ironically, the English were the first to reject the expanses of grass and woodland that this implied, and to seek to restore their gardens in the Renaissance manner. The consequence of their efforts was the creation of a peculiarly English neo-Renaissance style. Cecil Pinsent excelled in this field, and he was employed to create at least twenty private gardens in Tuscany. In 1908 he was commissioned by Berenson to redesign the garden at I Tatti.

Berenson lived at I Tatti for more than half a century, and it became a meeting place for intellectuals from all over the world. He described the house as 'a library with some rooms attached'. When he died, in 1959, he left the villa and his library to Harvard, his university. Berenson and his wife are both buried in the chapel beside the villa.

THE GARDEN

Pinsent created a Tuscan garden-in-miniature on the south-facing slope behind the villa. The site is cleverly divided by the old *limonaia*, which runs across the slope, effectively screening the lower garden, to create two substantial garden 'rooms'.

Pots of flowering geraniums stand on the broad terrace outside the villa. The ground slopes down

Villa I Tatti	
Nearest major town:	Florence
Advance booking:	Yes
Owner:	Harvard University
Address:	Via di Vincigliata, Settignano
Location:	Settignano lies to the north east of Florence. Follow the Via Gabriele d'Annunzio out of Florence. The Via Vincigliata is on the left of the road, just beyond Coverciano. The villa is situated on a sharp bend about ½ km up the road.
Open:	On written application to Harvard University at the villa. From April to June the villa is included in a garden tour organised by Associazione Toscana Agriturist, Piazza San Firenze 3, Florence, Tel: 055-287838
Admission:	Free, or L30,000 with Agriturist, including two other gardens, transport and tea.
Wheelchairs:	No
Refreshments:	No
Lavatories:	No

from the terrace towards the *limonaia*. A steep path creates the axis of the simple layout, which consists of a series of parterres arranged around four large persimmon trees. The central portion of the *limonaia* has been transformed into a covered terrace which overlooks the lower garden.

A double flight of steps runs down into the garden from the *limonaia*. A wall fountain set beneath the steps flows into a small pool. The lower garden is completely enclosed by hedges. It consists of a series of narrow terraces cut into the hillside. Each one is marked by an immaculately clipped box hedge. Between the hedges low, geometric parterres are laid out against a background of gravel. By excluding flowers from this area Pinsent was able to create his own version of the early Renaissance green garden. A flight of steps runs down from the pool, neatly balancing the horizontal lines of the terraces. The steps themselves are decorated with charming pebble mosaics, and flanked by obelisks of clipped box. Like the wide

hedges and parterres to either side of them, these obelisks represent Pinsent's own version of the Italian Renaissance style, although, if anything, they look more Elizabethan than Tuscan. A pool lies at the lowest level of the garden, and beyond it the view extends over open countryside.

A *bosco* below the formal garden creates a fine setting for statues. A cypress avenue runs through it, linking the villa to the lower entrance.

Villa I Tatti.

VILLA TORRIGIANI

SEVENTEENTH-CENTURY SUNKEN GARDEN AND POOL •
NINETEENTH-CENTURY ENGLISH LANDSCAPE GARDEN

HISTORY

Villa Torrigiani was built in the sixteenth century for the Buonvisi. During the seventeenth century it passed into the Santini family. Marquis Niccolò Santini, Lucca's ambassador to the court of Louis XIV, chose the villa as his summer residence. The south façade was rebuilt in the ornate style of the High Renaissance, and gardens were laid out around it. To the front of the villa, parterres were arranged around two large pools. To the rear, a fountain formed the focus of the parterre garden. An oblong pool and a sunken garden were laid out to the east of the villa.

In 1816 Vittoria Santini married into the Torrigiani family. Shortly afterwards the gardens were uprooted to make way for an 'English' park. Only the sunken Garden of Flora and the oblong pool above it survived.

Villa Torrigiani: the Garden of Flora.

THE GARDEN

A magnificent cypress avenue frames the entrance to the villa. The ornate façade of the building rises out of a sea of grass. Two irregular pools are the only remnant of the seventeenth-century parterres that once lay in front of it.

Like so many Tuscan gardens of the sixteenth and seventeenth centuries, Torrigiani's garden was built on an intimate, almost domestic scale. This is the principal charm of the sunken Garden of Flora, which lies to the east of the villa. The small rectangular space is completely enclosed, and acts as a sun trap in winter. It is linked to the upper terrace by a graceful flight of balustraded steps, built in perfect proportion to the garden.

In the seventeenth century gardens were still being designed as a setting for social events, and it is delightful to see them being used in this way today. When we were there, the regular beds of the sunken garden were being planted with marigolds in preparation for a family wedding. The gardener had been allowed some help for the occasion.

A nymphaeum is set into the retaining wall beneath the steps, and from it a straight path, decorated with pebble mosaic, leads to the Temple of Flora at the far end of the garden. By orchestrating innumerable *giochi d'acqua*, the marquis could chase his unwary guests into the garden from the upper terrace. Once there, they would find their escape route cut off by a wall of spray. As they retreated down the path, they would discover that this too was riddled with sprays. Dripping and breathless, they might seek shelter in the Temple of Flora, only to realise that this was the climax of their host's entertainment. The temple is really a grotto surmounted by a cupola. Flora stands on top of it, with delicate wrought-iron flowers at her feet. The gardener is willing to demonstrate the *giochi d'acqua* inside the temple, and the experience will be enlightening to anyone unfamiliar with the robust nature of seventeenth-century humour. Water, pouring simultaneously from the domed ceiling and the mouths of four statues representing the winds, was guaranteed to soak you to the skin. Additional jets used to rise from the floor, but the pipes froze and burst during the bitter winter of 1985. They cannot be mended without disturbing the mosaic, which naturally has a preservation order on it.

A graceful oblong pool lies above the sunken garden. It is shaded by trees and decorated with pots of lemon trees and statues. Water pours from the mouths of two masks set into the balustrade at the far end.

Villa Torrigiani	
Nearest major town:	Lucca
Advance booking:	No
Owner:	Contessa Simonetta Colonna Torrigiani
Address:	Camigliano, Lucca
Location:	Camigliano is approx. 14 km north east of Lucca. Take the ss435 for Montecatini Terme from the centre of Lucca. Camigliano is signposted to the left after approx. 11 km, just beyond Borgonuovo. Follow the road through Camigliano. The villa is well signposted from the village.
Open:	9-12, 2.30-6
Admission:	Garden only L2500 villa and garden L4000
Wheelchairs:	Yes, with assistance
Refreshments:	No
Lavatories:	No

VICOBELLO

SIXTEENTH-CENTURY TERRACED GARDEN

HISTORY

Vicobello was designed for the Chigi by Baldassare Peruzzi in 1576. When building work finished in 1580, Peruzzi laid out gardens on the steep south-facing hillside overlooking Siena.

Much of the original layout was destroyed during the eighteenth century, when an additional terrace was built beyond the boundary wall below the villa. However, it is known that the lemon garden, with its delightful exedral apse, was part of Peruzzi's design.

When seen from Siena, the garden was said to resemble the 'sei monti', or six mountains of the Chigi family crest. It may be that Peruzzi's terraces, piled one on top of the other and decorated with arched *berceaux*, did resemble the crest's jelly-mould form, which can be seen all over the garden.

The existing layout at Vicobello is of the simplicity typical of Tuscan gardens. The terraces are linked by modest flights of steps, and no attempt has been made to make architectural use of the sloping site.

The villa still belongs to the Chigi family, and has been designated a national monument.

THE GARDEN

Unlike many villas of the sixteenth century, Vicobello does not form the focus of a grand entrance avenue. The road leading up from the gatehouse is flanked by limes, but it runs parallel to the villa, and continues beyond the inconspicuous gateway that serves as the principal entrance. The gateway is marked by a small, semi-circular piazza which extends to one side of the road. The wall that encloses it is decorated with busts and lined with stone seats. Steps cut through the rows of square-topped ilexes that run across the hillside below. Below the trees there is a level lawn bordered by an ilex hedge. It is thought that this originally served as a bowling green.

Once inside the courtyard that lies in front of the villa, you can look back through the arched gateway at ilexes framing a lovely view of hills and open country. They conceal the new hospital that is being built immediately below.

The courtyard is enclosed on one side by the villa, and on the other by a string of buildings that once served as stables, servants' quarters, cellars and coach houses. A well stands between columns against the wall to one side of the gate.

At its northern end the courtyard is bounded by a walled *bosco* laid out to either side of an avenue of planes and chestnuts. A retaining wall isolates the area from the hillside below. This was a common security in those uncertain times.

Vicobello: the limonaia.

The lemon garden lies at the other end of the courtyard. It is bounded on one side by the *limonaia*, and on the others by clipped yew and box hedges. Peruzzi's beautiful apse is framed by cypresses on the far side of the garden. Its curving inner wall is decorated with niches, and two Roman busts stand to either side of the roof, which has the ubiquitous family crest at the centre.

A path runs down the centre of the garden, and lemon trees of an incredible size adorn the parterres that lie to either side of it. Their impressive terracotta pots are decorated with garlands. Some of the trees are over 300 years old. The fruit is unusually good – a single lemon is said to produce half a glass of juice.

Gateposts adorned with the family crest flank the entrance to the fruit garden that lies on the terrace below. Some of the fruit trees stand in parterre beds, others are espaliered against the brick wall of the upper terrace. Two oval fishpools, with wide stone rims, stand among the parterres at either end of the garden.

The narrow terrace below the fruit garden is shaded by a massive cedar which was planted in 1620. Azaleas fill the garden with a blaze of colour throughout the spring, and twenty different varieties of orchid hang in baskets from the trees. You would think that the lemon trees and orchids alone would provide enough work for the gardener, who manages to maintain the garden single-handed. He does, however, need help for the twice-yearly job of shifting the lemon trees. The largest pots need eight men to lift them.

A tunnel cuts through the boundary wall at the far end of the terrace and leads to the eighteenth-century flower garden. It is guarded at both ends by grotesques, and *spugne* adorn the walls. The greenhouse just inside the entrance once served as a geological museum, containing specimens from all over Tuscany. Beds of brightly coloured annuals are arranged around the enormous ginkgo tree that stands at the centre of the garden. A small balcony, set into the retaining wall on the far side of the terrace, affords a fine view over Siena.

Benevolent lions guard the steps that lead out of the flower garden. The Chigi crest, fashioned out of topiary, dominates the narrow terrace above. Another flight of steps leads up towards the villa. A fountain set into the retaining wall, and decorated with stalactites, serves as an overflow –

it only plays when there is too much water in the cistern that lies beneath the upper terrace. The villa and the family chapel stand side by side on the upper terrace, which is adorned only with simple circular beds of bright flowering annuals.

Vicobello	
Nearest major town:	Siena
Advance booking:	Yes
Owner:	Marchesa Ginevra Chigi-Bonelli
Address:	Via Vicobello 12, Vico Alto, Siena
Location:	Just north of Siena. Leave town centre on the Via Garibaldi. Turn right over the railway at traffic lights just before the station, following signs for 'Camping'. Follow dual carriageway for approx. ½ km. Turn left immediately before going under bridge. In order to do this you will have to turn round and come back down the other side of the dual carriageway. The avenue to Vicobello is the first turning to the left. The villa is on the left at the top of the hill.
Open:	By appointment throughout the year – letter or telephone
Admission:	Free
Wheelchairs:	No
Refreshments:	No
Lavatories:	No

EMILIA-ROMAGNA AND LE MARCHE

Emilia-Romagna, the northernmost of these two regions, and stretching as it does from the Apennines to the Po, has a wide variety of climate and landscape. Its name derives from the great Roman road that crosses it, the Via Aemilia.

Few gardens accessible to the public survive here. We have selected one in Ferrara, for it was in this city that the Este family established one of the most brilliant courts of the Renaissance. It was also an Este who created the magnificent garden at Tivoli, and who laid out the grounds of the Quirinal Palace in Rome.

The golden age of Ferrara ended in 1598. The heir presumptive, Cesare d'Este, was the natural son of his father. Pope Clement VIII, seeing his opportunity, issued a hasty Bull disallowing inheritance to illegitimate children. Papal forces then evicted the Este, and the city was left to decay under a remote Vatican administration.

The quiet region of Le Marche lies on the eastern slopes of the Apennines, and is mainly devoted to farming. The winters can be extremely harsh. The Apennine barrier meant that its cultural influences were Venetian rather than Roman.

The remarkable survival of the gardens in Le Marche is often attributed to the 'conservative nature' of its inhabitants. Whether or not one chooses to accept this generalisation, it is certainly credible that this remote Adriatic region should have been isolated from the changing fashions that wreaked havoc in the gardens of northern and central Italy. As a result the region represents a treat for garden travellers. The *giochi d'acqua* and water-powered automata of the villas Buonaccorsi and Caprile act as a key to understanding the humour of the eighteenth-century garden.

Giardino Buonaccorsi.

PALAZZO DI LUDOVICO IL MORO

EARLY SIXTEENTH-CENTURY PARTERRE GARDEN • MAZE

HISTORY

The Palazzo di Ludovico il Moro was built between 1495 and 1503. The project was commissioned by Antonio Costabili, Ferrarese ambassador to the Milanese court. The Duke of Milan at that time was Ludovico Sforza, il Moro (the Moor), which is presumably why the palazzo incorrectly bears his name. It has been said that Ludovico had it built as a bolt-hole after the invasion by Charles VIII of France. This theory is plausible, especially as Ludovico's wife Beatrice was the daughter of Ercole d'Este, but documentary evidence does not support it.

The palazzo was designed by Biagio Rossetti, the principal Ferrarese architect under Ercole I. Since 1492 he had been working on the 'addizione erculea', the carefully planned expansion to the north of the city. In addition he was responsible for the building of no less than eight palaces and four churches throughout the city. This enormous pressure of work perhaps explains why the palazzo was never completed (two sides of the courtyard remain unfinished).

The palazzo left the ownership of the Costabili with the passing of Este rule, and has changed hands many times over the centuries. In 1920 it was acquired by the State in a ruinous condition, and was restored during the 1930s. It currently houses the archaeological museum.

THE GARDEN

The garden is found on the far side of Rossetti's uncompleted courtyard. It is roughly square. The palazzo forms one side and part of another, while the remainder is walled. As you stand under the arcade, you see in front of you a row of four large rounded cones of yew, whose shapes echo the graceful curve of the arches above you.

The original design of the garden is not known. However, as it stands it is purely Renaissance in style, and we can safely assume that the earliest garden would have looked very like this. The designer has made maximum use of the limited space available by repeatedly dividing and subdividing the area with hedges of yew and box, separated by narrow gravel paths. There is an actual maze in the centre of the garden, but the overall effect is of one enormous labyrinth.

The garden is divided roughly into three by two shady avenues running the length of it. One is of

Palazzo di Ludovico il Moro	
Nearest major town:	Ferrara
Advance booking:	No
Owner:	The State
Address:	Via XX Settembre 124, Ferrara
Location:	The palazzo is in the south east corner of the city not far from the Porta Romana
Open:	All year 9-4. Closed Mon and national holidays
Admission:	Free (garden only)
Wheelchairs:	Yes
Refreshments:	No
Lavatories:	Yes

pollarded limes, and the other is a dense tunnel of roses. At an intersection in the rose tunnel there is a well. This has a fine Venetian well-head carved with acanthus leaves and there is ornate wrought-iron decoration on the support for the pulley. At the far end of this most peaceful of urban gardens, filled with the sound of wood-pigeons, rises a screen of tall cypresses.

Palazzo di Ludovico il Moro.

GIARDINO BUONACCORSI

EIGHTEENTH-CENTURY GARDENS • AUTOMATA

HISTORY

This wonderful garden, for many years designated a national monument, seems still to exist in the eighteenth century. The outside world has largely ignored it, few people have written about it, and its history is mostly unknown.

The villa was built in 1540. A garden must have been laid out at the same time, although there is no record of it. It is possible that the remarkable stone-edged parterres on the upper terrace are relics from this period. The style made its appearance at the end of the fifteenth century, although examples of it are very rare in Italy today. An eighteenth-century painting, which used to belong to the family, shows the garden almost exactly as it now appears. While it is generally accepted that the garden was laid out afresh at this time, we feel that the style is really that of the previous century. Perhaps the alleged conservatism of Le Marche accounts for this.

The new wing and terrace were added on the occasion of the marriage of the late Count Buonaccorsi in 1910. His widow maintained the house and garden with loving care until her death in 1979. Fortunately for the future of the garden, its new owners have announced their intention of undertaking a full programme of restoration. We hope that they may also find an assistant for the devoted and capable gardener, who has worked there for the last 30 years.

THE GARDEN

The garden consists of five terraces descending from the villa. The upper three are almost exactly as they were during the eighteenth century, even down to the lemon trees that are espaliered along their walls. Considering that they have to be covered against frost for several months each winter, this exemplifies the devotion with which the Buonaccorsi tended their garden over the centuries.

You enter the garden onto the highest terrace, which acts as the *giardino segreto*. It consists of four stone-edged parterres each divided into a variety of geometrical shapes – stars, lozenges, etc. The colourfully planted parterres contain potted lemon trees and eccentric little obelisks with ball feet. A pool in the centre of the terrace is surrounded by theatrically dressed putti, and a number of Venetian figures complete the scene. The use of Venetian statues in this garden demonstrates how Le Marche looked to Venice rather than Rome or Florence for cultural inspiration. The Apennines were more than simply a physical barrier.

The family chapel is at one end of the terrace. Almost hidden behind a huge clipped cypress hedge, it resembles a small man wearing an outsize false beard. At the opposite end of the terrace, steps lead down to a small courtyard beside the villa. The garden wall here is decorated with mosaic and has a niche containing a figure of Pan.

Giardino Buonaccorsi: the water-powered huntsman.

Continuing round the front of the villa you will find the aviary, decorated with tufa and occupied by a number of canaries. A fountain plays inside it.

Beneath the villa, at the end of this path, lies a grotto. Inside, a life-size monk is at prayer, while another looks in horror at the devil, whose wooden head pops out from a hole in the rock as you enter. *Giochi d'acqua* in the ceiling would once have guaranteed you a drenching.

The second terrace contains a number of simple parterres, with citrus trees espaliered against the retaining wall. Four elaborately carved obelisks stand along the central path.

The third terrace is narrower than the others. It is known as the *Viale degli Imperatori* from the imperial busts that line it. It is, in effect, a simple gravel walk, where you may stroll without the risk of being mocked by the grotesque dwarves and *commedia dell'arte* figures who populate the other terraces. At one end stands a nymphaeum occupied by Flora, the presiding deity of the garden. She is crowned with a star whose points once sprayed water. From the nymphaeum a *berceau* runs back up to the chapel. It is densely covered in a wonderful tangle of ivy, jasmine and Russian vine.

The fourth and fifth terraces were probably planted at a slightly later date than the others. The fourth contains simple rectangular parterres that are a mass of colour during the summer. The retaining wall is set with wall fountains and covered with valerian and climbing roses. Stone benches are arranged on this level so that you may rest and look not at the view but back at the garden above you.

The lowest level consists of a series of private shaded walks between high laurel hedges, where you come across deep lily pools alive with frogs. In the centre of the high boundary wall that ends this terrace, is one of the garden's many extraordinary survivals. This is the collection of water-powered automata, which stands in a small shell-covered grotto. In the centre a life-size wooden huntsman sits on a rock, his hunting-horn at this lips. Behind him in niches are a Turk, a harlequin and a little group of smiths around their forge. Their mechanisms are still intact, and they are even clothed in faded and tattered eighteenth-century costumes. They are almost the only surviving examples of their kind, and we look forward to seeing them fully restored by their owners.

Further along the wall you reach the capacious *limonaia*, with its built-in stoves as a necessary precaution against the cold Marche winters. Immediately beyond this you enter the nineteenth-century *bosco*. This has been carefully landscaped in the Romantic manner, and on a hot day it is pleasant to wander among the full-grown ilexes and the Venetian statues. There is a series of pools and cascades (dry at the time of writing) and at one point the path spirals up a mount, although the view from the top is now obscured by trees. Eventually the path leads back into the garden below the chapel.

Giardino Buonaccorsi	
Nearest major town:	Ancona
Advance booking:	Individuals no, groups yes
Owner:	Società Agripicena
Address:	Via del Giardino 9, Potenza Picena
Location:	Potenza Picena is about 30 km south of Ancona. Follow signs to the garden from the centre of Potenza Picena. It is several km; when in doubt stick to the main road. On arrival it is signposted as Ristorante La Villa and Ristorante Il Fauno.
Open:	All year, 8-12. On arrival go through the arch to the left of the villa. Follow the wall until you reach the garden gate. Ring the bell, have patience, and the gardener will admit you.
Admission:	Free
Wheelchairs:	No
Refreshments:	Two restaurants, booking advised
Lavatories:	Yes

Giardino Buonaccorsi.

VILLA CAPRILE

EIGHTEENTH-CENTURY GARDEN • WORKING
GIOCHI D'ACQUA

HISTORY

Since the fifteenth century the wealthy families of Pesaro had built summer residences on the slopes of the Colle San Bartolo above the city, following the lead of the Sforza at Villa Imperiale. Villa Caprile began its life as a hunting lodge belonging to the Mosca, a local family. In 1640 Marchese Giovanni Mosca began to turn it into a more substantial building. In 1763 Francesco Mosca had the villa considerably enlarged by Carlo Marchionni, and over the next twenty years the gardens took on their present form. The 'green theatre', with seats clipped from cypress, was constructed at this time, although little remains of it today.

From 1817 to 1818 the villa was occupied by Princess Caroline of Brunswick and her paramour Bartolomeo Pergami. In 1876 it was acquired by a school of agriculture, and in 1934 it became a State Agricultural Institute. During the Second World War the villa was used as a strongpoint on the Gothic Line, and was badly damaged in consequence. The occupying Germans also felled the cypress avenue to give a clear field of fire. It was replanted immediately after the war, but, sadly, these trees are now diseased, and they are again to be felled and replaced. A general programme of restoration is underway, with assistance from the provincial administration of Pesaro.

THE GARDEN

The garden of Villa Caprile consists of three descending terraces directly in front of the villa. The highest terrace, protected on three sides by its retaining walls from the bitter Marche winds, is planted with parterres in box and myrtle. These are filled with annuals. This is not traditional but is done here, one of the staff told us, to please the visitors. As far as is possible, the Institute grows plants traditional to this garden; plumbago, bougainvillaea and old roses, among many others. They are aided in this by the extremely sheltered nature of the garden and the huge underground spring-fed reservoirs that were dug when the

house was first rebuilt. The gradual cooling of the climate, however, has meant the loss of a number of species, among them acacia and a 100-year-old China tree (*Kolreuteria paniculata*) over 30 feet high.

Beneath the steps leading down to this terrace lie several grottoes. The central one, flanked by dolphins whose eyes spurt water, is decorated with mosaic and *spugne*. Visible through a hole in the rock are a number of little figures, solemnly rotating. Water can spray out from a star in front and also from the metal flower in the ceiling. Immediately to the right is the *grotta dell'orologio*, where water sprays from the clock inside. To the left of the central grotto lies yet another, occupied

Villa Caprile: the devil in the grotto.

by a labyrinth of pipework and carefully labelled stopcocks. Here the controller of the *giochi d'acqua* stands, able to watch his guests' reactions through a peephole into the next grotto. The entire length of the retaining wall has been fitted with pipework and sprays, so there is no safe position. Even the forewarned, leaning over the balustrade to watch their friends' discomfiture, could be soaked by water jetting upward from the balustrade itself.

Further along the wall to the right is the most beautifully decorated of all the grottoes. Two small alabaster busts guard the entrance. The floor inside is mosaic, while walls and ceiling are of *spugne* inset with shells in a delicate pattern. Razorshells have also been used; their mother-of-pearl surfaces give a lustrous glow to the interior. Even in this setting, however, you are not safe from the robust humour of the garden designer. A wooden hatch flies open to reveal the devil, complete with pitchfork. You are invited to touch him for luck. Needless to say, on doing so water jets from his mouth and, for good measure, from floor and ceiling as well.

In the centre of the terrace the fountain was once in the form of a great metal globe. It is now thickly covered with mosses and ferns, creating a strangely beautiful effect.

There are two seats at the head of the steps leading to the next terrace. Should you be so misguided as to pick the wrong one, you will find yourself firmly clamped to your seat, while jets of water strike you in the face.

The lower terraces were undergoing massive restoration while we were there, and it was not possible to visit them. They contain two large fountains, one showing Atlas bearing the world on his back. The other has a metal ball bobbing on a jet of water above an iron basket. The lowest terrace was the original fruit and vegetable garden, and is now planted with scented shrubs.

We very much look forward to revisiting this garden when the restorations are complete. We also hope that these will include the removal of the hideous lamp-standards that line the cypress avenue.

Villa Caprile	
Nearest major town:	Pesaro
Advance booking:	No
Owner:	Istituto Tecnico Agrario Statale 'A. Cecchi'
Address:	Via Caprile 1, Pesaro
Location:	From centre of Pesaro follow signs to Rimini, ss16. On the outskirts of the town the Institute is signposted to the right.
Open:	July, Aug 3-7.30. Guided tours given by students from the college.
Admission:	L2000, children L1000
Wheelchairs:	No
Refreshments:	No
Lavatories:	Yes

Villa Caprile: the interior of the grotto.

VILLA IMPERIALE

UNIQUE SIXTEENTH-CENTURY HANGING GARDEN

HISTORY

The earliest house on this site, which still exists and forms part of the present complex of buildings, was erected by the Sforza during the first half of the fifteenth century. The villa received its name after a visit, in 1452, by Emperor Frederick III to Alessandro Sforza, then Governor of Pesaro.

By the 1520s the house was owned by Francesco Maria Della Rovere, Duke of Urbino, and his wife Leonora Gonzaga. In 1522 they began a huge programme of reconstruction. Rome was by now the leader in architectural design, and the ducal architect Girolamo Genga is known to have been influenced by Raphael. Masson describes the duke giving Genga one of Raphael's letters in which he sets out his ideas for Villa Madama.

Following the complete redecoration of the old house, the new villa was constructed and gardens laid out on the hillside above the site. The resulting building was for many years one of the most famous in Italy.

During the seventeenth century the Della Rovere line died out and the villa passed by marriage to a branch of the Medici family. It was no longer occupied and fell into decay. Severe damage, sustained during the Second World War, might have seen the end of it, had it not been for the dedicated attention of its present owner.

THE GARDEN

From a distance it is the old fifteenth-century building, with its tall watchtower, that predominates. As you approach, the ingenuity of the construction becomes apparent. Connected to the earlier building by a bridge, the newer villa lies between it and the steeply rising ground beyond. At either end it extends narrow wings into the hillside on which the garden is laid out. The result is a central courtyard enclosed on three sides by the villa and overlooked on the fourth side by terraces. As well as the intended design for Villa Madama, this also recalls Bramante's plans for the Cortile del Belvedere in the Vatican, begun in 1505.

From the villa a shady portico opens into the courtyard. This is now laid out with eight rectangular beds, bordered with pebbles and planted with annuals. All around you rise walls set with scores of niches containing terracotta urns and amphorae whose colour harmonises perfectly with the pale brick.

Spiral staircases and passages in each of the wings to left and right lead to the first terrace. This contains the *limonaia* and several simple parterres. Its walls are densely covered with wisteria. You would think that this terrace alone would provide enough work for the single gardener employed here.

Villa Imperiale	
Nearest major town:	Pesaro
Advance booking:	Organised tours only
Owner:	Conte Guglielmo Castelbarco
Address:	Strada di San Bartolo, Pesaro
Open:	One organised visit weekly during the summer months only. Apply to: Azienda di Soggiorno, Via Rossini 41 Pesaro, Tel: 0721 69341
Admission:	L4000 (includes transport)
Wheelchairs:	No
Refreshments:	No
Lavatories:	Yes

Climbing further up the stairs brings you out in one of a pair of loggias in front of the upper garden. The topiary this once held has long since vanished, and the present owner has replanted it as a parterre garden, ornamented with potted lemon trees. The walls are still covered with potted lemon trees. The walls are still covered with espaliered fruit trees, as they were originally. The semicircular loggias in the corners, which gave access to the surrounding *bosco*, have disappeared.

Returning to the front of the terrace, a balustraded walk runs along the top of each connecting wing to two more loggias at each end of the villa. The view from these is superb.

Villa Imperiale.

LAZIO

The history of Lazio (Latium) is effectively the history of Rome. In turn, the period that concerns us is largely dominated by the deeds of the papacy.

It was not until 1417 that the papacy was firmly re-established in Rome, following the turbulent events of the thirteenth and fourteenth centuries. During the following years the influence of the Tuscan Renaissance began to make itself felt. By the end of the century Roman artists and architects had devised their own distinctive style. Both spiritual and temporal rulers were to make full use of it.

The importance of the Roman Renaissance in garden design lies in its recognition of the fact that a garden could create a specific visual effect. This could be done by the use of perspective, changes of level and an axial layout. From being a place of retreat where man drew consolation from nature, the garden became a place of display, where nature was at the service of man. This understanding of the malleability of landscape lies at the heart of all subsequent garden design.

Villa Lante.

VILLA ALDOBRANDINI

EARLY BAROQUE GARDEN • LARGE WATER THEATRE • WATER STAIRCASE

HISTORY

Villa Aldobrandini was built between 1598 and 1603 for Cardinal Pietro Aldobrandini. He came of a Tuscan family, which achieved prominence when Ippolito Aldobrandini was elected to the papacy as Clement VIII in 1592. His first act was to bestow a cardinal's hat on his nephew Pietro.

In 1598 Pietro acted as his uncle's strong-arm man in the eviction of the Este from their city of Ferrara. As a reward for this the Pope bestowed on him not only the revenues of the Duchy of Ferrara, but also an estate above Frascati, which he had seized the previous year. A simple villa already stood on the site. This had been erected in the 1560s by Pier Antonio Contugi, doctor to Pius IV. The cardinal commissioned Giacomo della Porta to design the new villa, which incorporated much

of the earlier building. After della Porta's death in 1602, the villa was completed the following year by Carlo Maderno with the assistance of Giovanni Fontana. In 1603 the cardinal persuaded a neighbour to allow him water rights over his land, and built 8 miles of aqueduct and canal to bring water to his garden. The great waterworks it was to supply were designed by Orazio Olivieri, who had been curator of the fountains at the Villa d'Este.

Pietro found little favour with his uncle's successor, the Borghese Pope Paul V. His Ferrarese revenues were stopped, and in 1610 he was placed under house arrest. He died without an heir in 1621, and the property passed to his cousins, although a trust had been established to preserve the family name. Ironically, it was a Borghese who assumed the title of Prince Aldobrandini during the last century.

The villa and gardens were badly damaged by Allied bombing during the Anzio landings. They have since been restored by the owners, although much work remains to be done.

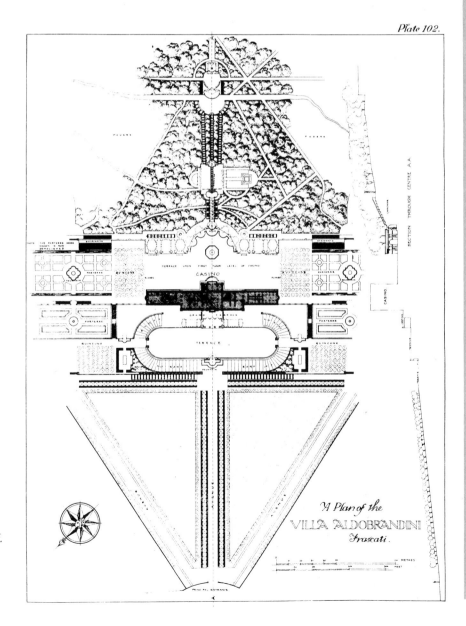

Plate 102.

Left: *Villa Aldobrandini: the plane quincunx.*

Right: *Villa Aldobrandini.* The Art of Garden Design in Italy, *Triggs,* 1906. *(Bodleian, 19187 b.6.)*

135

THE GARDEN

This enormous villa towers above the little town of Frascati. It was originally approached from the entrance in the middle of the town, and must have grown ever more impressive as you made your way up the ilex-shaded central avenue. To either side stretched a broad *tapis vert*, with two further avenues running diagonally to each end of the villa.

Now, however, the gates stand rusted shut as they have for more than a century, the ilexes have grown into an impassable tunnel, and the *tapis vert* is no more than a rough pasture. The present entrance is from the steep lane to the left. This brings you onto the great oval terrace below the villa. From here, ramps lead both to an upper terrace and down to join the original entrance avenue. Two grottoes are placed on the central axis; one at the head of the avenue, the other at the back of the oval terrace.

From the upper terrace a door in the wall to the left of the villa leads into the garden. It opens into a grove, more correctly perhaps a quincunx, of ancient pollarded planes, whose huge grotesque forms are straight out of Arthur Rackham. Originally a large parterre garden lay beyond this, but it no longer exists. The pattern is repeated at the other end of the villa, where the parterres still survive, and the plane grove is filled with large hydrangeas. The cultivated areas of the garden are well maintained by a staff of ten.

Between the groves, opposite the villa, is the garden's famous 'water theatre'. Several authors have found this feature disproportionately large for the narrow space behind the villa. We agree, although it is undeniably impressive. In the centre stands Atlas, water pouring over him from the globe he bears. At his feet the buried Titan, Enceladus, struggles for freedom. (He is said to be imprisoned beneath Sicily, hence its frequent earthquakes.)

According to one of Falda's seventeenth-century illustrations, Atlas was once aided here by Hercules. This would have been a dual allusion. Firstly, to the legend of the Hesperides, to which reference is made in the other decorations of the theatre. Secondly, to Pietro Aldobrandini's assistance to the Pope in the matter of Ferrara, which is also mentioned in the inscription around the top of the theatre. Falda's work is not always to be relied upon, however; his curious identification of Pan, on the left of the theatre, as the one-eyed Polyphemus, is a case in point.

In a niche on the other side there is a horn-playing centaur. This, and Pan, are relics of an extraordinary orchestra which played a variety of water-powered instruments under the direction of Apollo. All the other figures have now vanished, which would have pleased Président de Brosses. After his visit to the villa, in 1740, he commented, 'What can be more chilling than to see these stone creatures, daubed with colour, making melancholy music without piping or moving?' He may, of course,

Villa Aldobrandini	
Nearest major town:	Rome
Advance bookings:	No
Owner:	Prince Aldobrandini
Address:	Via Massaia 18, Frascati, Roma
Location:	Frascati is 20 km south east of Rome on ss215. Enter the main piazza, with the villa visible above it, and you will find Via Massaia in the top left-hand corner.
Open:	Mon–Fri, 9–1. Entrance tickets available *only* from the Azienda di Soggiorno, Piazza Marconi 1, Frascati, Tel: 9420331
Admission:	Free
Wheelchairs:	Yes, as far as the water theatre
Refreshments:	No
Lavatories:	No

have been feeling disgruntled after being soaked through twice in one day by *giochi d'acqua*. It is interesting to note that the statues were originally polychrome.

The two chambers to left and right are, respectively, a chapel dedicated to St Sebastian, and the 'Room of the Winds'. The latter once continued the theme hinted at by the 'orchestra', with a representation of Mount Parnassus, home of the Muses, and a statue of Pegasus. John Evelyn's famous description also mentions a 'copper ball that continually dances about three foot above the pavement by virtue of a winde conveyed secretly to a hole beneath it'.

The broad stone terrace above the theatre is reached by a sloping ramp. From here there is a fine view of the villa, with the Apennines lining the distant horizon. Immediately above the theatre the line of the central axis continues with a steep water staircase. At its head it is flanked by two tall columns. Their summits shoot out jets of water, which then fall back into the runnels that spiral down their sides like fairground helter-skelters.

There are two further cascades above this point. The steps are dangerous and the climb is steep, but it is worth making, for it is here that the major differences between this garden and its predecessors are best appreciated. The first point is that the villa is intended to be the centrepiece of the garden, and so blocks the view that, in an earlier garden, would have been left open. The second difference is the rapid transition, within the boundaries of the garden, from an artificial to a rural landscape. This was originally symbolised by the highest cascade, known as the Fountain of the Shepherds (mostly destroyed during the Second World War). Simple rides trail off into the *bosco* that presses closely in on either side.

Villa Aldobrandini. Le Fontane delle ville di Frascati nel Tuscolano, *Falda, 1675. (Bodleian, Arch. Antiq. B.1.3.)*

SACRO BOSCO
VILLA ORSINI, VILLA BOMARZO
SIXTEENTH–CENTURY MANNERIST FANTASY GARDEN IN WOODLAND SETTING

HISTORY

The Sacro Bosco, or 'sacred grove' was built by Pier Francesco 'Vicino' Orsini It has been attributed to many different artists over the years, but it seems most likely that Orsini himself planned the park, and then hired sculptors and a team of labourers to bring his ideas into being.

Work began in 1552. As a soldier in Pope Paul III's army, however, Orsini was away from home almost continually until 1567. He fought in Germany, Flanders and the Papal States, and spent two years as a prisoner of war. It was only when he retired at the age of 54 that he was able to devote himself entirely to the park.

Orsini was not a powerful man in the political sense, however he was an important figure in the intellectual world, and moved freely among the educated men of his day. As the husband of Giulia Farnese he became an *habitué* of her cousin's palace in Caprarola, and also numbered Cardinal Gambara of Villa Lante among his friends. The Sacro Bosco gave expression to all these different aspects of his life. In it he gave three-dimensional form to his love and knowledge of literature and his personal philosophy. He also took the opportunity to mock the pomposities of his more illustrious friends.

Orsini continued to work on the Sacro Bosco until he died in 1584. When all the statues were complete, he amused himself by painting them in bright colours. Although the park was famous during his lifetime, when he died it fell almost at once into obscurity. It seems that it was never visited by any of the great travellers and diarists of the seventeenth and eighteenth centuries. In 1645 the property was sold to the della Rovere, and in 1845 it was sold by them to the Borghese, who bought it as part and parcel of some agricultural land.

The fortunes of the Sacro Bosco changed dramatically in 1949 when it was visited by Salvador Dali. He found the place in ruins. The large statues were completely overgrown, and the smaller ones were strewn about the woods. Dali's visit brought the park back into the public eye. Three years later the University of Rome undertook the massive job of piecing together the original layout, and seeking out the archival material that would help them in their task. In 1954 Signor Giovanni Bettini bought the site, and has since devoted himself to its restoration.

THE GARDEN

The Sacro Bosco is best seen on a winter's day in the middle of the week. Then it is deserted and the statues stand abandoned among the fallen leaves, making it possible to catch something of the mysterious mood that Orsini wished to create. During the summer the park draws crowds of tourists and school children. They destroy the atmosphere, and the statues too, judging by the 6 foot high chain-link fences which protect them.

Vicino Orsini lived at a time when it was becoming fashionable to convert the family stronghold into a Renaissance villa, and to lay out gardens in place of fortifications. Orsini's palace can still be seen perched on a cliff high above the park. He bowed to fashion to the extent of creating a small terraced garden below it. However, his real enthusiasm was reserved for this rocky slope a ¼ of a mile away. Here he planted trees to create his sacred grove, and then had a phantasmagoria of statues and monuments hewn out of the lumps of tufa that lay scattered around the site. When it was complete, the park could just be seen from the north-facing apartments of the palace.

Sacro Bosco: the tilting house.

Such was the power of the local legends that grew up around Orsini's monsters that, in 1980, an altar was erected in the park and an official exorcism performed. However, it seems unlikely that Orsini intended to frighten his visitors, who would have been able to 'read' his creation rather as we might read a book today. His theme was man's journey through the snares and passions of the world to an understanding of divine love. Broadly speaking, this idea has been explored by both Petrarch and Dante, who had laid the foundations for the literature of the Renaissance. It was a theme that Orsini could explore in relation to his own life, thereby creating in the park a kind of personal monument. He chose to use the extraordinary figures that people the pages of 'Orlando Furioso' as a vehicle for his message, and many of the statues can be identified in the context of Ariosto's epic poem. For an exhaustive account of the iconography we recommend Margaretta Darnall and Mark Weil's study.

Orsini's voice is audible in every corner of the park, in the form of the inscriptions that are picked out in red paint on the lichen-covered stone. Many of them acted as keys to an interpretation of the place, and could be traced back to Dante, Petrarch and Ariosto. Others were the words of Orsini himself who, like a good story-teller, constantly reminded his visitors of the extraordinary nature of what they were seeing.

The park was laid out on three levels, with the Temple of Divine Love at the top. Visitors originally entered by way of a small bridge over the stream at the bottom. The towering figures of the two struggling giants would have been the first things they saw. The fact that one was tearing the other apart by the legs would have alerted them to the fact that they were witnessing a scene from 'Orlando Furioso'. (In his madness, Orlando rent a woodcutter in two.)

Entering by way of a new bridge further up the stream, you will pass the end of an avenue of fountains leading to a huge open-mouthed mask. The mask marks the point where the stream enters the garden. It is surmounted by the globe and castle of the Orsini family crest, which are cut out of the living rock.

Continuing past the giants to the lowest level of the garden one is greeted by an extraordinary sight. Here, a huge moss-covered tortoise supports

Sacro Bosco: the gryphon.

a statue of Fame blowing a trumpet. To the modern eye this odd combination of images has rather the effect of a collage. However, contemporary visitors would have recognised it immediately as the well-known aphorism of *festina lente*, or 'make haste slowly', which was formed by the combination of almost anything with a tortoise.

Beyond the tortoise, a statue of Pegasus on a rock rises out of the tilting bowl of a fountain which once poured water into the stream below. Pegasus was a familiar symbol among the rich and the great. From his hoofmark on Mount Helicon the spring of the Muses flowed into their gardens. Villa d'Este at Tivoli exemplifies Pegasus' role in drawing attention to the owner's prowess as an intellectual and a patron of the arts. By placing the fountain at the lowest level of the garden, in absurd juxtaposition to the tortoise, Orsini succeeded in mocking the pomposity of Ippolito d'Este and others like him.

Continuing on the same level, one arrives in a shady grove. The stone seats that stand to each side of the path are large enough to accommodate two people – they are lovers' seats. A bas-relief set into the hillside on the left shows the Three Graces, with their bottoms in high relief. Beyond them is the remains of a nymphaeum, which was once enclosed and contained a fountain surrounded by cupids. This area represents an earthly paradise, from which the visitor must free himself in order to follow the higher calling of divine love.

A clearing beyond the grove is the site of a theatre, formed by a curving wall set against the slope. The niches once held statues, and the top of the wall was decorated with a balustrade. The remains of it can be seen in the undergrowth below the clearing, near the bowl of an unfinished fountain.

At one end of the clearing Orsini built a dramatically leaning house. The simple building's only decoration is a bear, or *orso*, holding the Orsini arms and shield. It is said that the house was built to reveal the corrupt nature of the world; when you stand on its sloping floor all the momuments outside appear to tilt.

A long terrace lies above the clearing, on the second of the park's three levels. It is lined with enormous urns that are not unlike Etruscan funerary vases. This level is peopled with a selection of extraordinary figures, each one imbued with its own significance. At one end there is a colossal female figure with a vase on her head. She is sometimes said to represent lasciviousness, on account of her voluptuous form and the image of two harpies torturing a man, which is carved on her broad back.

The shallow pool at the end of the terrace is guarded by a river god, not dissimilar in appearance to those at Villa Lante. The colossal female figure to his left may represent Angelica, the object of Orlando's unrequited passion. A dog stands guard over her recumbent form.

To the right of the fountain there is a gryphon locked in mortal combat with two lions. No one has managed to fit the elephant that stands below them into a credible iconographic account of the park. Clad in the full regalia of war, it squeezes the life out of a Roman soldier with its trunk.

The Hell Mouth, perhaps the most famous of the monuments, is also on this level. It forms part of a monstrous face, with flared nostrils and staring eyes. A flight of steps leads into the mouth where a stone bench and table seem to suggest that it would be a good place for a picnic. The structure was built to amplify and distort sound, and it is said that the voice of anyone inside can be heard all over the park.

On the third and highest level Orsini built his own version of the hippodrome that had recently been excavated at Hadrian's Villa. Giant acorns and pinecones decorate the edges, while the oak tress that stand to one side of it send down a shower of real acorns throughout the autumn. The area is guarded by fish-tailed harpies, lions and bear cubs that hold the Orsini arms and rosette. Cerberus sits under a nut tree at one end.

The Temple of Divine Love stands on a slope above the hippodrome, representing the ultimate goal for travellers through the garden. Its simple structure is decorated with Orsini rosettes and Farnese lilies. The door mouldings are made from parts of the Etruscan tombs that were found on the site. Orsini dedicated the temple to his wife on her death, and the present owner has followed his example.

Sacro Bosco (Villa Orsini, Villa Bomarzo)	
Nearest major town:	Viterbo
Advance booking:	No
Owner:	Sig. Giovanni Bettini
Address:	Parco dei Mostri, Bomarzo
Location:	Well signposted from the centre of the town.
Open:	Mon–Sun, 8–5 throughout the year
Admission:	L6000/L5000 children under 10
Wheelchairs:	No
Refreshments:	Yes
Lavatories:	Yes

VILLA BORGHESE

SEVENTEENTH–CENTURY VILLA AND MUSEUM • LARGE LANDSCAPED PARK

HISTORY

In 1605 Cardinal Scipione Borghese began to buy land on the Pincian hill just north of the Roman city walls. Born Scipione Caffarelli, he had been made a cardinal by his uncle, Pope Paul V, on condition that he took the family name. A gentle and generous man, known as the 'delight of Rome', he was also a collector of considerable wealth and taste. The villa, or casino, was never meant to be lived in. It was designed as a gallery for his collection, much of which is still there to be

Left: *Villa Borghese. The Art of Garden Design in Italy, Triggs, 1906. (Bodleian, 19187 b.6.)*

Right: *Villa Borghese: the aviary.*

THE
VILLA BORGHESE
ROME

seen. Initially he commissioned Flaminio Ponzio as the architect, however he died almost immediately, and the work was taken over by Van Santen, a Utrecht architect known in Italy as Giovanni Vansanzio. The casino was completed by 1616, and Girolamo Rainaldi was called in to lay out the formal gardens around it, between 1617 and 1619. It is likely that he was also responsible for the charmingly frivolous baroque aviary. Pietro Bernini created most of the garden sculpture.

Very little of the seventeenth-century garden survives. In about 1789 all of the grounds were relaid by Jacob Moore, a Scottish painter resident in Rome, who was a protégé of the Prince Borghese of the time. He laid out the hippodrome, the lake and possibly also the Temple of Aesculapius, although some authorities date this to a later remodelling of the gardens in 1849.

Shortly after completion of the villa a plaque was erected at the main garden entrance. The Latin verses on it read, in part, as follows:

I, custodian of Villa Borghese on the Pincio, proclaim the following: Whoever you are, if you are free, do not fear here the fetters of the law. Go where you wish, pluck what you wish, leave when you wish. These things are provided more for strangers than for the owner . . .

This was not always heeded by the owners. A first attempt to close the park had failed in 1828. A later generation of Borghese, hoping to sell off most of the land to developers, were taken to court and defeated by the municipality of Rome in 1885. Rights of access were awarded on four afternoons a week. In 1902 the family, bankrupted by building speculation, were forced to sell the estate to the republic for three million lire.

Rainaldi's gardens are now in a sorry state. The casino is currently being restored, and work is not scheduled to begin on the gardens until it has been finished. This is likely to take a number of years.

THE GARDEN

Villa Borghese was the first of the great Roman parks intended for public enjoyment, and it still serves that function. It is the 'green lung' of Rome, covering an enormous area and densely wooded. It is this that makes it so pleasurable to wander in and explore.

The casino was built in a corner of this huge park. It had its own small formal gardens which still survive, although in very poor condition. The secret gardens lie on either side of the casino, and there is a *parterre de broderie* garden immediately behind it. The balustrade set with fountains, which encloses the rear garden and the front courtyard, is a twentieth-century copy. The original was sold to Viscount Astor in 1896, and may now be seen splendidly relocated along the great terrace at Cliveden in Buckinghamshire. The entrances to garden and courtyard are guarded by herms.

There is an aviary at the end of the narrow secret garden to the left of the casino. It is equipped with four wrought-iron domes which rise most oddly above the baroque pediments. The narrow strip of formal garden extends in a straight line into the park. On the far side of the aviary there is a small dining pavilion. Beyond this the garden slopes gently downwards, overlooked by a balustraded terrace. Fruit trees are espaliered against the retaining wall.

Little else remains of the original layout. Rainaldi's open-air theatre survives to the north west of the casino, and Bernini's herms look down at the old chestnut-sellers. The regular pattern of paths and groves, with a fountain or statue at each intersection, has been replaced by meandering paths and broad avenues. Moore's 'English' garden covers the western end of the park, with its lake (where boats may be hired) and classical temple. It is nonetheless an enjoyable place to wander in at a weekend to watch the endlessly entertaining procession passing on horseback, bicycles, rollerskates and sometimes even on foot.

Villa Borghese	
Nearest major town:	Rome
Advance booking:	No
Owner:	The State
Address:	
Location:	The Villa Borghese is in the huge park of the same name in central Rome. The nearest Metro station is 'Flaminio'. The park is also crossed by several bus and tram routes. Buses nos 202/203/205/490/495. Trams nos 19/30.
Open:	7–dusk
Admission:	Free
Wheelchairs:	Yes
Refreshments:	Yes
Lavatories:	Yes

VILLA D'ESTE

SIXTEENTH–CENTURY GARDEN FAMOUS FOR ITS FOUNTAINS

HISTORY

The Villa d'Este was built in about 1555 by Pirro Ligorio for Cardinal Ippolito d'Este. Ippolito was the younger son of Alfonso I of Ferrara and his wife, Lucrezia Borgia. A man of enormous ability and great wealth, he was not only a generous patron of all the arts but a knowledgeable and sensitive collector and antiquarian. It is said that it was his notorious ambition that finally denied him the papacy. When Julius III was elected in his place on a split vote, he offered Ippolito the governorship of Tivoli in gratitude.

The governor's residence at Tivoli was the old Franciscan monastery. On his arrival in 1550, Ippolito immediately began its transformation. He commissioned Ligorio, who was at that time his Director of Antiquities, responsible for the excavation of the nearby Villa Adriana (Hadrian's Villa). Work on the gardens began in 1560 and was completed by 1575.

Ippolito died in 1572. He left the property to any future cardinals of his family. Should there be no suitable heir, the villa was to go to the Dean of the College of Cardinals. On his death his nephew, Cardinal Luigi d'Este, inherited. However, when Luigi died, in 1586, there was no Este cardinal and the property went to the Dean, Alessandro Farnese, an old Este rival. Before he could take possession, however, the Este stripped villa and garden of everything movable. When, in 1605, the villa was returned to Cardinal Alessandro d'Este, the garden statuary was returned, but by then Ligorio's subtle iconographical design had been hopelessly confused.

The decay of the gardens began during the eighteenth century. In 1787 the villa fell into Austrian hands through the marriage of Beatrice, last of the Este, into the Hapsburg family. Like so many Hapsburg properties in Italy, it was then completely neglected.

After the First World War the villa became the property of the Italian Republic. The gardens were restored. During the Second World War the villa and gardens were heavily damaged by bombing, but have since been restored again. The number and complexity of the waterworks means that constant maintenance has to be carried out. This is well performed. The planting, however, has been allowed to become much thicker than it would once have been.

THE GARDEN

Once upon a time coaches would arrive in Tivoli and leave their occupants at the bottom of this garden, to make their own way up to the house. Unfortunately, the present entrance is through the villa. We would advise you to go straight down through the garden, looking neither to right nor left, until you reach the little gate at the far end of the central axis. Now turn round, and you will see it (more or less) as the designer intended, with the steep forested slope ascending to the villa. The basic plan of the garden is simple: a central axis, on which you are now standing, with the two principal cross-axes running across it at right angles.

It is important to understand that the whole garden was designed to glorify the cardinal not just by its magnificence, but also by the use of a symbolism easily comprehended by any educated person of the sixteenth century. We will describe later how this functioned.

The passage you are in is thought to have been covered by a pergola. This was designed in the form of a cross centred on the cypress 'rotunda' in front of you, where there stood a grand octagonal pavilion. This no longer exists (if it ever did) and the rotunda is currently being restored to its seventeenth–century state. When completed it will frame a view of the villa.

On the wall to your right is the fountain of the many-breasted Diana (Artemis) of Ephesus. A copy of a classical original in the Farnese collection, she was considered, in the sixteenth century, to represent Mother Nature. (She was also the divinity who gave St Paul so much trouble during his mission to the Ephesians.)

This is the flattest part of the garden, and

consists of a number of simple square parterres. Originally it was planted with fruit trees and herbs. The two curious little hillocks standing to your right are called the *'metae sudantes'*, and are miniature versions of the fountains that stood near the Colosseum in ancient Rome. They were intended to be placed in the central fishpools; thankfully this was never done.

The three great rectangular fishpools form the first main cross-axis of the garden. Their still waters reflect the roaring turbulence of the Fountain of Neptune at the far end. This fountain was a simple cascade until 1927 when it was transformed by the addition of a number of powerful jets. A continual rainbow hangs in the spray that surrounds it.

Above this great cataract stands the Organ Fountain, constructed in 1568. This originally held the statue of Diana and was known as the Fountain of Nature. The organ itself was based on classical designs described by Vitruvius. Water pressure was used to make it produce musical notes and even trumpet-calls automatically. The baroque portico behind it dates from 1611.

The ascent from the first cross-axis rises steeply towards the villa. It is climbed by means of three parallel staircases. The central stair is flanked by a descending water 'chain'. To its right is the stair of the *'Bollori'* (boiling water). The steps are flanked by masks, all different, which spout water into basins where it is ingeniously made to froth and bubble.

The central stair ascends to the Fountain of the Dragon, where it divides and climbs in two beautiful curves around the fountain to the terrace above. The fountain represents the many-headed dragon Ladon, who guarded the entrance to the Gardens of the Hesperides. A huge statue of Hercules, who vanquished Ladon, once stood in the niche behind the fountain. From the curving inner balustrades water spurts high into the air before dropping back into the pool beneath. Down the outer balustrades flow streams of water that gush from the breasts of a pair of sphinxes on the terrace above.

This terrace forms the second main cross-axis. It is known as the Path of the Hundred Fountains, and is perhaps the best-known feature of the gardens. Three parallel channels run along it, one above the other. The highest channel is fed by boat-shaped fountains and ornamented with fleur-de-lis, eagles and obelisks. Hundreds of little animal masks pour water from one level to the next. It was decorated with terracotta reliefs of Ovid's *Metamorphoses*, but these have mostly disappeared, either decayed or concealed behind the dense mat of ferns that droop into the channels.

At the left-hand end of the path is the Oval Fountain. It is situated in a shaded courtyard equipped with stone tables and benches. It is hard to imagine a more beautiful place to dine on a summer's day. The air is cooled by the great cascade that pours into a large oval pool. Nymphs on either side continually empty their urns into the water. A path runs behind the pool, with arches which permit you to look out from behind the tumbling water. On top of an artificial mound above the cascade there is a statue of Pegasus leaping into the air. There is an empty grotto to one side of the courtyard, which was once the Grotto of Venus.

At the opposite end of the path is the Fountain of the Rometta (Little Rome). A fountain in the form of a boat lies in front of a raised stage. In the centre of the stage there is a statue representing Rome, with Romulus, Remus and the wolf to one side. To the left rises a curious collection of miniature buildings. These once extended all along the back of the stage, and were intended to be replicas of the monuments of classical Rome. Most of them, however, fell into the valley below during the last century.

Below the Rometta lie two other fountains. One (under restoration at the time of writing) is dedicated to Proserpine. It was originally known as the Fountain of the Emperors, and held statues of the four Roman emperors known to have lived in the vicinity. The other is called the Fountain of the Owl. It once contained a display of mechanical birds whose water-powered song continued until an owl appeared whose hooting frightened them into silence. It is now a simple fountain in a niche decorated with the Este eagle and fleur-de-lis. Its columns are beautifully entwined with mouldings of the apples of the Hesperides.

At the very top of the garden, immediately below the retaining wall, runs another transverse path. This is called the Cardinal's Path, and runs from the grotto of Aesculapius to the marvellous Grotto of Diana at the right-hand end. This is magnificently decorated with bas-reliefs of mythological acts of chastity: Diana and Actaeon, Perseus

Above: *Villa d'Este: the central pools.*

Previous page: *Villa d'Este: a detail from the Path of the Hundred Fountains.*

and Andromeda, Apollo and Daphne and others. It was once also occupied by statues of Diana, Minerva and Hippolyta, which are now in the Capitoline Museum.

Finally, returning along the Cardinal's Path, you can climb the last steps to the central loggia and enjoy the magnificent view over the valley. Beneath your feet the line of the central axis is completed by two last fountains; that of Pandora and, below her, Bernini's 'Bicchierone', or 'goblet'.

The garden symbolism mentioned earlier has been skilfully analysed by D. R. Coffin in *The Villa d'Este at Tivoli*. There are three principal themes. The first concerns nature and art, and is developed along the two cross-axes. Thus, on the lower axis life-giving waters stem from Mother Nature, fill the fishpools and irrigate fruits, vegetables and flowers. It was originally intended to build a Fountain of the Sea at the far end of the fishpools. This was to contain a statue of Neptune and would have received all the waters of the garden. The upper axis, relating to art, begins where the hoof of Pegasus has struck out the spring sacred to the Muses. It flows to the Rometta, representative of man's greatest achievements.

The second theme also follows the upper axis. The Oval Fountain is to be recognised as representing the real cascades of Tivoli. The three channels down which its water flows are the three local rivers which eventually join the Tiber at Rome, thus linking the locations of the cardinal's greatest achievements.

The final theme is the most important. This is based on the Este claim to be descended from Hercules. Thus Hercules is made the presiding deity of the garden. His statue, standing as it did midway between the grottoes of Venus and Diana, illustrated his legendary choice between vice and virtue. Having chosen the virtuous path, he won the apples of the Hesperides, emblematic of temperance and chastity, which are here repeatedly shown to be in the possession of the Este eagle. In this way the entire garden glorifies both the cardinal's virtues and his ability to transform nature into art.

Villa d'Este	
Nearest major town	Rome
Advance booking:	No
Owner:	The State
Address:	Villa d'Este, Tivoli
Location:	Tivoli is east of Rome on the ss5 (or take the A24 and the Tivoli exit). The villa is easily found in the centre of the town. Note that it will be crowded on summer weekends, and parking will be difficult.
Open:	Jan 9–4, fountains play 10–1, 2–4.30 Feb 9–5, fountains play 10–1, 2–5.30 Mar 9–5.30, fountains play 10–1, 2–7 Apr 9–6.30, fountains play 10–1, 2–7.30 May–Aug 9–6.45, fountains play 10–1, 2–7.30 Sept 9–6.30, fountains play 10–1, 2–7.30 Oct 9–4.45, fountains play 10–1, 2–5.30 Nov 9–4.15, fountains play 10–1, 2–5 Dec 9–4, fountains play 10–1, 2–4 Closed Mon. Exit 45 mins after closing time.
Admission:	L5000
Wheelchairs:	No
Refreshments:	Yes
Lavatories:	Yes

PALAZZO FARNESE

BEAUTIFUL SIXTEENTH–CENTURY GARDEN • CASINO • WATER STAIRCASE

HISTORY

In 1504 Cardinal Alessandro Farnese bought the area of countryside in which Caprarola lies. Following the sack of Rome by Spanish troops in 1527, he decided to build a secure place of refuge in the town. He commissioned Antonio da Sangallo, who began work in about 1530, and was assisted by Baldassare Peruzzi. In 1534, however the cardinal was elected to the papacy as Paul III. His attention was drawn away from Caprarola, and it was not until after his death, in 1549, that work was to continue there.

One of the Pope's first acts had been to make a cardinal of his fourteen–year–old grandson, another Alessandro. In 1556 the younger Alessandro commissioned Vignola to transform his uncle's partly built fortress into a palace befitting the more settled times. Work began on the gardens behind the palazzo the following year, and in 1559 construction of the building itself got underway.

The sophistication and luxury of the palazzo were unparalleled, earning Alessandro a firm rebuke from Cardinal Carlo Borromeo. Told that the money would have been better spent on the poor, Alessandro (with a readier wit than his colleague at Villa Lante) replied to the effect that he had indeed given the money to them; they had earned it by the sweat of their brows.

Vignola died in 1573. One of the twin secret gardens was finished, and the palazzo nearly so. It is not certain whether Vignola himself planned the creation of a further garden in the hunting wood behind the palazzo. At all events, in 1584 the cardinal proceeded to build a delightful casino there, some of whose waterworks strongly recall Vignola's work at Bagnaia. The casino was probably designed by Giacomo del Duca. It was finished in 1586, three years before Alessandro's death. It is pleasant to think of him enjoying this enchanting place in his old age.

In 1620 the gardens around the casino were laid out afresh by Rainaldi. His alterations included the

rustication of the stonework, and the addition of the grottoes and the *canephori*. He brought in Pietro Bernini to carve these.

The last of the Farnese died in 1731, and Caprarola passed to the Bourbons. They stripped it of its contents and left it to decay. In 1940 it was bought by the State, and the casino later became an occasional residence for the President of Italy.

THE GARDEN

This enormous building towers over the town of Caprarola. At first sight it is difficult to imagine a garden that would not be crushed into insignificance against a background of such overwhelming grandeur. The solution found to this problem was brilliantly simple. The main gardens were to be sufficiently distant from the palazzo for there to be no conflict of attention. It is a pity that we do not know to what extent Vignola was responsible for this plan. Certainly del Duca carefully followed Vignola's work at Villa Lante, both in the design of the waterworks and of the casino itself.

The palazzo is pentagonal in plan. The two square *giardini segreti*, for which Vignola was definitely responsible, lie behind it, each parallel to a different facet of the pentagon. The whole building is roughly aligned on an east-west axis. As was customary, the cardinal had two sets of apartments. One was for winter use and faced south, the other, facing north, was for the summer. Each set of rooms overlooks one of the gardens and is connected to it by a wooden bridge over the moat that surrounds the palazzo.

After guiding us through a maze of stairs and passages, a custodian showed us through the cardinal's dressing room and into the garden facing his winter apartments. Since the Second World War this has been replanted in the original pattern, with four green parterres surrounded by hedges of box, holly and laurel. A central avenue (once covered by a pergola) leads to the Fountain of the Rain in a grotto at the far end of the garden,

Palazzo Farnese: the
canephori.

where water drips from the roof and the faces of satyrs emerge from the *spugne*-covered walls. In front of it the Farnese lily is laid out in mosaic. Above the grotto there is a balustraded terrace.

The garden facing the summer apartments was closed for restoration while we were there. It originally contained flowerbeds and fruit trees. A nymphaeum at the far end was occupied by the Fountain of Venus. Between the two *giardini segreti* there is a raised terrace around which runs a rose pergola.

From the summer garden a path leads up into the hunting wood. As you stroll across the turf in the shade of the ancient chestnut trees, the formality of the palazzo behind you is forgotten. It is now that the garden springs its most delightful surprise. The path becomes a straight grassy pine avenue. In a sunny clearing at the far end the casino rises up in perfect harmony with its sylvan setting. It stands at the top of a short slope and is reached by a flight of shallow steps that run between rusticated walls. Down the middle of the steps runs a water staircase composed of intertwined dolphins. Grottoes are set into the retaining walls on either side.

Walking up the steps, with the sounds of water echoing from the walls on both sides, you find yourself in the small piazza at the head of the water staircase. Stairs sweep up and around the central fountain to the terrace above. The fountain is an extraordinary creation. Two enormous tritons, bearing cornucopias, flank an urn as vast as any at Bomarzo. The urn is filled with water from a jet in the form of the Farnese lily. The water overflows into a lower basin, around the rim of which are set bowls from which spring further jets. There is a grotto behind the basin.

As you climb the curving stairs, you will notice wall fountains in the form of grotesque masks set into niches beside you. At the top there is a small piazza. On either side the Farnese unicorns spout water into shells borne by kneeling tritons. Beyond the piazza lies the large rectangular terrace around the casino. It is planted as a formal garden with box parterres. On the low wall running around the terrace stand a number of tall *canephori* – 28 altogether. Each has a vase on its head, and some hold animals in their arms. The pair at each corner face each other and hold hands. There is a charming story to the effect that each one is a

portrait of one of the workmen employed in the construction of the garden.

Flights of steps on either side of the casino, decorated with water-spouting dolphins, lead up to the last terrace behind it. Here there is a fountain surrounded by shallow mosaic steps. The Farnese coat-of-arms is also laid out in mosaic. Beyond the fountain three low terraces recede towards the woods. They are planted with roses, and the retaining walls are set with numerous fountains which, sadly, no longer function. Finally, a gate, decorated with nymphs astride unicorns, opens into the forest outside.

Palazzo Farnese	
Nearest major town:	Viterbo
Advance booking:	No
Owner:	The State
Address:	Caprarola, Viterbo
Location:	Caprarola is about 19 km south east of Viterbo. Follow signs for Ronciglione. After about 15 km turn off to Caprarola; the palazzo is conspicuous in the centre of the town.
Open:	9–4, closed Mon. It is necessary to ask specifically to see the casino, which is a little distance from the palazzo. You will be accompanied by a custodian.
Admission:	L2000
Wheelchairs:	No
Refreshments:	No
Lavatories:	Yes

VILLA LANTE

WELL-PRESERVED SIXTEENTH–CENTURY GARDEN •
FINE WATER STAIRCASE • FOUNTAINS

HISTORY

Bagnaia, in the diocese of Viterbo, was for long a place of retreat and recreation for its bishops. At the beginning of the sixteenth century the forest above the town, known as Monte Sant'Angelo, was enclosed to form a hunting wood. In 1514 the first building on the site, a small hunting lodge, was erected. This still stands in the park. In 1549 an aqueduct was built to convey water to both park and town.

In 1566 Cardinal Giovanni Francesco Gambara was appointed to the bishopric. It is almost certain that he commissioned Vignola, then working at Caprarola, to draw up the design for his new residence.

The garden was completed by 1573. Both *palazzine* were included in the original plan. The first was completed and occupied by 1578. In 1579, however, Gambara's allowance was stopped. This was probably on the intervention of Cardinal

Villa Lante. The Art of Garden Design in Italy, *Triggs, 1906. (Bodleian, 19187 b.6.)*

Plate 118.

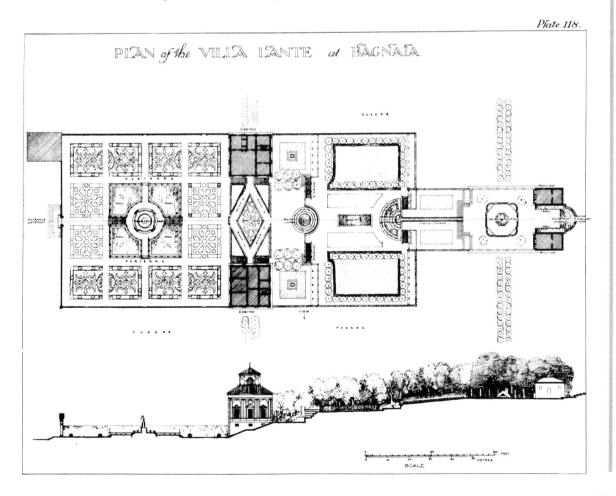

Carlo Borromeo, whose austere, if saintly, nature is known to have been offended by the lavish spending of many of his colleagues. The creation of beauty was, in his view, no part of the proper function of a prince of the Church. On the cardinal's advice, Gambara went no further with his plans, and built a local hospital instead.

In 1587 Gambara died, and the Vatican immediately took over the property. It was rented to his successor on the condition that, on his death, it should be left to the current Pope's nephew, Cardinal Montalto, who inherited in 1590. He proceeded to build the second *palazzina* and to make minor alterations to the layout of the garden. These included the great central fountain, to which he added the figures of the four Moors supporting the Montalto crest.

In 1640 work had begun in Rome on a new series of fortifications. This resulted in the loss of most of the garden of the villa belonging to the Lante family. In compensation they asked for the villa at Bagnaia, still owned by the Holy See. In 1655, they were granted the lease on a peppercorn rent, which eventually lasted for 200 years. They were given the freehold during the last century. In the seventeenth century a French member of the family was responsible for the *parterres de broderie* around the central fountain, which were originally simple square beds.

The Lante left the villa in 1932. In 1953 it was bought by Angelo Cantoni, who made good the considerable war damage and brought the garden to its present wonderful condition. It is now owned by the State.

THE GARDEN

Villa Lante has a well-deserved reputation as the most beautiful of all the Roman gardens. Its modest scale, its symmetry, which is perfect without being daunting, and its hundred variations of running water under the shade of its great plane trees, all combine to make it an unforgettable experience.

Like many Roman estates, Villa Lante was intended for public as well as private enjoyment. Thus it has two entrances, one directly into the parterre garden and the other, for general use, into the park that surrounds the garden (and was once an extension of it). You now enter through the second gate. Set into the rising ground inside is the Fountain of Pegasus, who is emerging from an oval balustraded basin. From the wall behind, herms spurt fine jets of water into the pool.

Just as at Tivoli, the garden of Villa Lante might have been read as easily as a piece of narrative verse by the sixteenth-century eye. Unlike the Este garden, however, the symbolism does not glorify an individual, but retells the tale of man's ascent from the Golden Age to the age of civilisation, as recounted in Ovid's *Metamorphoses*. Briefly, the park represents the free but primitive Golden Age, although the statues which indicate this have nearly all been lost or changed. Following this age came the Flood, just as the water flows from the park to the Fountain of the Deluge. From here the water runs under the control of a great crayfish (a *gambero*, the cardinal's personal emblem). Further on Tiber and Arno, overlooking the dining terrace, make the land fruitful. The formal garden at the lowest level demonstrates the synthesis of nature and art. (For a detailed account, see Coffin, *The Villa in the Life of Renaissance Rome*.)

A flight of shallow steps to the left of the Fountain of Pegasus leads up to the gate into the lower garden. This is square, and contains *parterres de broderie* set around a large square pool. There is a circular island in the centre, reached by balustraded bridges from each side. On the island stand the travertine figures of four Moors holding aloft the Montalto crest, surmounted by a star spraying water. Four stone boats float on the pool, each manned by arquebusier from whose weapon further jets of water once sprang.

The garden continues up the slope between the twin *palazzine*. The right-hand one is the earlier, erected by Cardinal Gambara, and was used as the owner's residence. The Montalto *palazzina* was for formal receptions. Between the *palazzine*, paths lead up to the next level. The Fountain of the Lights is set into the retaining wall, resembling a flight of steps to the next level. Jets of water rise like candlesticks from little stone dishes along each step, hence its name. Grottoes to either side, under restoration at the time of writing, belong to Neptune and to Venus.

The next level forms the 'dining room' of the garden. The view from here is magnificent, looking out over the parterre garden with the roofs of the town behind it, and beyond that to open countryside stretching to the horizon. In the centre of the terrace stands a long stone table with a channel cut down its length, through which fresh water flows. Too high to sit at, the table was presumably used to cool wine after the imperial Roman fashion. Behind the table is the Fountain of the Giants. These are the gods of Tiber and Arno (strongly resembling the Neptune at Bomarzo) who overlook the pool at the base of the fountain. Water overflows into the pool from a central basin supported by a triton. This, in turn, is fed by the claws of an enormous crayfish, whose limbs border the water staircase above. They stretch all the way to the next terrace, where the mouth of the *gambero* pours out water between them.

Hedges enclose the uneven steps on either side of the water staircase. You emerge into a box-walled enclosure lined with stone benches. In the centre is the three-tiered Fountain of the Dolphins. *Giochi d'acqua* around the base of the fountain are still in use.

Behind this, great plane trees line the approach to the head of the garden. So old that many of them are little more than hollow trunks, they still cast a delightful green shade over the terrace. Behind them lies the last fountain, that of the Deluge. It is a tall fern-filled grotto, with a central cascade pouring into a pool where two mossy dolphins swim. Enclosing it on either side are the two charming Pavilions of the Muses, frescoed inside with birds, flowers and musicians. There is a small *giardino segreto*, filled with roses, to the left.

Villa Lante	
Nearest major town:	Viterbo
Advance booking:	No
Owner:	The State
Address:	Bagnaia, Viterbo
Location:	Villa Lante is signposted clearly from Viterbo, following the ss204 towards Orte. Bagnaia is 4 km east of Viterbo. In the central piazza (XX Settembre) in Bagnaia take the middle of three roads to the right (Via Gianbologna). The villa is at the end.
Open:	Nov–Feb 9–4 Mar 9–5.30 Apr 9–6.30 May–Aug 9–7.30 Sept 9–6.30 Oct 9–5.30 Accompanied tours of the garden every half-hour.
Admission:	L2000
Wheelchairs:	No
Refreshments:	No
Lavatories:	No

VILLA MADAMA

SIXTEENTH–CENTURY GARDEN DESIGNED BY RAPHAEL

HISTORY

Despite the Villa Madama's brief and turbulent history, its importance to Roman garden architecture cannot be overestimated. It was one of the earliest buildings in which a return to the ancient Roman tradition was consciously attempted. Though incomplete, its influence can be traced in almost every subsequent Renaissance design.

The work was commissioned by Cardinal Giulio de'Medici. The plans were drawn up by Raphael, and work began early in 1519. Following Raphael's death in 1520, it was continued by his colleagues, Antonio da Sangallo, Giulio Romano and Giovanni da Udine. Work stopped the following year when the cardinal was compelled to return to Florence, and was not resumed until 1524, after his election to the papacy as Clement VII. Within a couple of years the villa was on the way to completion, and was already a meeting-place for the learned and the amusing among the Pope's acquaintance.

Disaster struck in 1527, when Rome was brutally sacked by Emperor Charles V's Spanish army, which ran riot after the deaths of its generals. The villa was burned almost under the eyes of its unhappy owner, who was effectively a prisoner in Castel Sant'Angelo. Though Clement later made good the damage to the building, he went no further. Too many of the friends with whom he had once enjoyed it lay murdered. It remains today as it stood before the sack.

On Clement's death, in 1534, the villa was left to Ippolito de'Medici. When he died all his properties were confiscated by Pope Paul III. In 1539 it passed to the Pope's grand-daughter Margaret of Austria, for whom it is named. In 1549 Paul III died and the villa was restored to the Medici. Six years later Catherine de'Medici, Queen of France, gave it to Cardinal Alessandro Farnese.

With the extinction of the Farnese line during the eighteenth century, Villa Madama passed into the hands of the Bourbons and a long period of ruinous neglect. The gardens were restored by a tenant at the beginning of this century, using Sangallo's original drawings. Since 1960 it has been owned by the State, and is now used to hold receptions.

Villa Madama: entrance to the hippodrome.

Villa Madama	
Nearest major town:	Rome
Advance booking:	Yes
Owner:	The State (Ministero degli Affari Esteri)
Address:	Via di Villa Madama, Roma
Location:	The villa lies at the end of the Via di Villa Madama, not far from the Olympic Stadium. This is in the north-west quarter of the city. It is not easily reached by public transport.
Open:	By prior arrangement through the Information Office at the villa. Telephone Signora Ortolani on 06–36911.
Admission:	Free
Wheelchairs:	Yes
Refreshments:	No
Lavatories:	Yes

THE GARDEN

Raphael's original plans drew heavily upon the younger Pliny's famous description of his own villa and garden. By following the ancient tradition, Raphael hoped to create a place where garden and building would merge without abrupt transitions from 'inside' to 'outside'. The villa was to be built, roughly speaking, as a square block enclosing a great circular open courtyard. Having entered from the south-east face, you would then have had the choice of three exits from the courtyard. Each would take you through the villa to reveal a different aspect of the gardens. To the left a Roman amphitheatre was to have been excavated from the hillside, while on the right the whole slope below the villa was to have been terraced. The villa was to lie at the junction of two perpendicular axes. The whole building was aligned with the Vatican to the south east. A road was to run straight to it from the Ponte Milvio, the line being continued through the amphitheatre to join the Via Trionfale at the summit of Monte Mario above the villa.

Only half of the building was completed, so that the wall of the central courtyard now forms the semicircular façade. Inside the villa you almost immediately find yourself in the great north-west loggia, which is most gloriously frescoed with scenes from Ovid's fables. These are the work of Giovanni da Udine, Giulio Romano and Perruzzi. The loggia is now glassed in to preserve the frescoes, but was originally open to the garden beyond.

This garden is known as the *Giardino della Fontana* and continues the axis towards the north west. It is filled with clipped box parterres in rectangular patterns. Recently an attempt was made by the gardeners to introduce colour into this dark area by planting roses, but the *soprintendenza* had them removed on the grounds that they were anachronistic. Three niches are set into the west wall of the garden. The central one contains Giovanni da Udine's elephant-head fountain, said to have been copied from a classical original. The opposite side of the garden is open to a magnificent view eastwards over Rome. Beneath the balustrade is a large oblong pool, fed by fountains in the retaining wall. The wall at the far end of the garden has a gate flanked by two enormous stucco figures by Bandinelli. Most of the garden statuary was looted during the Second World War, but

Villa Madama: the elephant fountain.

these were evidently rather too big for the 'collectors' to move.

The gate leads into the hippodrome, so called from a reference in one of the younger Pliny's letters, rather than from its function. Green parterres run down the centre, and long lines of cypresses create shaded walks down either side. The trees are suffering from the ubiquitous cypress disease, and are soon to be replaced. There is an eighteenth-century nymphaeum at the far end, which was being restored at the time of writing. The garden is a place of great peace and beauty, and is well cared for by the three gardeners. The curator, surely one of the happiest men in Rome, told us that nothing but the owls ever disturbed his night's rest.

GIARDINO DI NINFA

MAGNIFICENT TWENTIETH–CENTURY PLANT COLLECTION • MEDIEVAL RUINS

HISTORY

Pliny the Younger records a visit to the prosperous town of Ninfa in the first century AD, when a temple sacred to the nymphs stood over the spring of the River Nympheus.

By 1159 the town had seven churches, and was encircled by double walls. Its site on the road between Rome and Naples made it a popular stopping place. In 1297, at the height of its prosperity, it was acquired by Pietro Caetani, Duke of Caserta. He built the structure that still serves to dam the lake, and the tower that overlooks it.

The town continued to flourish until disaster struck in 1382. Onorato Caetani, who was embroiled in the events of the Great Schism, declared Clement VII antipope, and Ninfa was razed to the ground as a result. The few survivors who stayed on in the ruined town soon fell victim to malaria. What was left of their shops and houses, and the remains of the fortified walls that surrounded them, was abandoned until the early years of this century.

When Gregorovius, the German historian, visited it in the middle of the eighteenth century, he made the following comment: 'Truly this place looks even more charming than Pompeii, for there the houses stare like crumbling mummies dragged from the volcanic ashes. Over Ninfa waves a balmy sea of flowers'. Augustus Hare also referred to the flowers, which 'grow so abundantly in the deserted streets, where honeysuckle and jessamine fling their garlands through the windows of every house, and where the altars of the churches are thrones for flame-coloured valerian'.

The glorious garden that is now laid out among the ruins is a tribute to the loving care of three generations of the Caetani. Ada Wilbraham Caetani, Duchess of Sermoneta, began to build the garden with her son Prince Gelasio Caetani in 1922. By this time the site was so overgrown that the ruins were scarcely visible beneath the weeds. Having had the ground cleared, they planted plane trees, cypresses, ilexes and pines. Being of English origin,

Ada Caetani was particularly fond of roses. Many of the roses that she planted still flourish in the garden today. After her death, Roffredo Caetani and his American wife Marguerite Chapin continued to work on the garden. Their daughter Lelia was the last of the Caetani, and she and her English husband Hubert Howard devoted their lives to Ninfa. It is to them and their team of untrained gardeners that we owe the wonderful condition of the garden today. Hubert Howard also created a nature reserve in the surrounding area.

During the Second World War Ninfa was commandeered by the Germans, who used it as a munitions dump. The Caetani took refuge with other local people in the castle at Sermoneta. When they returned to Ninfa they found, happily, that the garden had survived largely undamaged.

Lelia Howard died in 1977. A trust, already created to protect the family property, took over responsibility on the death of Hubert Howard in 1986. The management of the garden was entrusted to Hubert's nephew Esmé Howard and Lauro Marchetti, who spend much of his childhood with the Howards and went on to work as their private secretary.

THE GARDEN

Ninfa was built on the banks of a river at the foot of the Lepini mountains. This proved to be a uniquely favourable position for the garden that has transformed the desolate ruins. The River Ninfa, which rushes through the garden with great force, is fed by snow water from the mountains. The plants thus thrive on copious supplies of water throughout the long hot summers.

The simple family villa was built by Ada Caetani out of the ruins of the medieval town hall. The garden stretches out in front of it, its shape defined by the course of the river, the ruins and the remains of the city wall. The Howards drew water from the river to create the streams that run all over the garden. Some of them intersect, forming

Giardino di Ninfa: medieval remains.

cascades which fill the place with the sound of water.

Ninfa contains over 10,000 species of plants, flowering trees and shrubs. The collection, which must be attributed largely to Hubert and Lelia Howard, could qualify as a botanical garden, although this was never the intention of the owners. They travelled widely, visiting parks and gardens all over the world, and collecting plants. Both of them were green-fingered, and they succeeded in acclimatising plants from Australia, South Africa, China, Japan, the Himalayas, and North and South America. The collection includes twenty varieties of prunus, innumerable acers and magnolias that have grown into massive trees. Orange, lemon and grapefruit trees abound, alongside malus, ceanothus and huge bushes of viburnum. Lelia Howard painted several pictures of the garden, and her canvases still act as an inspiration to those entrusted with its care. Its informal layout, lush lawns and grass paths have often earned it the title of an 'English' garden. The sight of the crumbling walls swathed in clematis, climbing roses and wisteria certainly arouses a pang in the heart of the English traveller abroad!

Today Ninfa is under threat. Industrial development is planned for the land that surrounds it. Perhaps more threatening still is the popular opinion that the garden's opening hours should be extended. At present public access is strictly limited. This has served as a protection against the institutional atmosphere that can so easily settle on a garden that is run by managers and not used by owners. Ninfa is already visited by 40,000 people each year. The grass paths and medieval bridges could barely withstand the impact of more visitors.

Giardino di Ninfa			
Nearest major town:	Latina	**Open:**	shortly before the garden entrance.
Advance booking:	No		Apr–Oct, first Sat and Sun of each month, 9–12, 2.30–6. (Jul–Sept, 3–6). Guided tours only. A limited number of tickets are sold each day. It is best to buy them in advance from the Fondazione Roffredo Caetani, Palazzo Caetani, Via delle Botteghe Oscure 32, Rome, Tel: 06–6543231 Open 8–6. Tickets may also be bought from the World Wild Fund for Nature, Via Mercadante 10, Rome, Tel: 06–8440108. Open 5–7 pm.
Owner:	Fondazione R. Caetani		
Address:	04010 Doganella di Ninfa		
Location:	Ninfa is approx. 70 km south east of Rome. Take either the ss148, which is quicker, or the ss7. From the ss148, cut across to Cisterna by turning left at Montello, approx. 55 km from Rome. From Cisterna follow yellow tourist signs for Ninfa. At Doganella cross the main road. The entrance to the garden is on the right after approx. 1 km. If you see the lake and medieval tower you have already passed the carpark, which is a field		
		Admission:	L6000 on site, L5000 in advance
		Wheelchairs:	No
		Refreshments:	No
		Lavatories:	No.

VILLA DORIA PAMPHILI

SEVENTEENTH–CENTURY CASINO, GARDEN AND PARK

HISTORY

In 1630 Pamphilo Pamphili bought a simple villa and some land on the Janiculan hills, just outside Rome. When he died, in 1639, he left a wife, Olimpia, and three sons. Olimpia was not a helpless widow. Almost as soon as her husband died, she began to lavish attention on his brother Cardinal Giambattista Pamphili. Such was her influence over him that when he succeeded to the papal throne in 1644, taking the title of Innocent X, she was dubbed 'the first *papessa* of Rome'. During Innocent's reign a decision was taken that allowed money from the Holy See to be used to enrich the Pope's immediate family. With Olimpia at the helm, the Pamphili were to benefit enormously during Innocent's reign. Camillo, one of Olimpia's sons, decided to transform the family villa into a residence that befitted their new status.

Camillo Pamphili's first choice of architect was Francesco Borromini. Sadly, Borromini's extravagant plans did not meet with Camillo's approval. His intention had been to create a series of walled avenues which could be flooded for a number of hours each day. He proposed that Pamphili's visitors should walk around the park on foot in the morning, and then retrace their journey by boat after lunch! Borromini was no doubt inspired by the convenient proximity of the city aqueduct. In the notes that accompanied his plans, he explained that they could be realised with little inconvenience to the citizens of Rome, who 'would only have to lose their water for an hour each day'. He also intended to build a replica of the ark. It was to be fitted with stalls, and live animals were to be purchased to live in it. (He admitted that life-size replicas would have to be substituted for some species.) A statue of Innocent X was to stand in the garden, so placed that, each day at the hour of his accession, a ray of sun would touch the tips of his toes.

Camillo eventually commissioned Alessandro Algardi and Giovan Francesco Grimaldi, who was a landscape painter. His original intention had been to extend the old villa. However, this idea was abandoned in favour of building the casino. The new building served as a setting for the Pamphili's extravagant receptions and parties. It also housed the family's considerable collection of classical sculpture. The old villa remained virtually unchanged, although Algardi laid out gardens and an orange grove around it.

G. B. Falda's engraving of 1683 provides an accurate record of Algardi's layout. The regular plantation of trees and hedges, which can still be seen in front of the casino's main entrance, formed the upper garden. The sunken garden to the rear of the building contained traditional geometric parterres arranged around a central fountain. It overlooked the lower garden, which was bounded by ilex woods and occupied by parterres, a large amphitheatre and an elaborate grotto set into the side of the hill. Beyond the gardens the vast park was intersected by a series of avenues flanked by hedges and statues.

By the end of the seventeenth century the Pamphili family was extinct, and the property passed by marriage to the Doria of Genoa. In 1720 Gabriele Valvassori was commissioned to design the Fountain of the Tiber and the Fountain of Venus, which were to stand outside the old villa. He also built a wall around Algardi's orange grove. Later in th eighteenth century the nearby villas of Ferroni and Corsini were annexed to the property.

Early in the nineteenth century Prince Doria took an English wife called Mary Talbot. (Gwendoline Talbot, her sister, was to marry the Borghese prince of the day.) Under Mary's orders much of Algardi's garden was uprooted, making way for an 'English' park. She put a signature to the completed work by having her name inscribed in clipped cypress on the eastern slopes of the park.

During the Siege of Rome in 1849, the park was witness to some ferocious fighting between Napoleon III's forces, intent on defeating the republican government, and an army drawn from the whole populace of Rome, under the military leadership of Garibaldi. A neoclassical memorial to the dead was erected beyond the family villa.

Before they sold the villa and park to the State in 1963, the Doria replaced all the fountains with copies, taking the originals with them.

THE GARDEN

The casino can be seen from the park's main entrance. It is a magnificent sight. The building is surmounted by a delicate balustrade, and its walls are decorated with ancient bas-reliefs set into pale stucco. From a distance it has a luminous and almost ethereal quality.

A path leads through the bleak periphery of the park and joins the carriage drive to the casino. The gate that marks the main entrance to the garden is closed, and one must follow the drive until it emerges beside the retaining wall of the sunken garden. Between the flights of steps that linked the two gardens you will see the sad remains of Algardi's grotto of Venus. The wall is decorated with the doves and lilies that were the emblems of the Pamphili.

The sunken garden is not open to the public, however a marvellous view may be obtained by climbing the steps to the terrace above it. The garden is enclosed on one side by the villa, and on the others by the retaining walls of the upper terraces. Niches set into the walls are adorned with statues. The *parterres de broderie*, which replaced the original geometric beds, probably date from the end of the seventeenth century. They are set out around a copy of a fountain by Pietro Tacca. Pots of lemon trees decorate the outer wall of the garden and the oblong pool that lies to one end of it. The pool also contains bronze fountains in the form of Pamphili lilies. Ducks and geese swim on it, and a tree grows on a circular island at its centre.

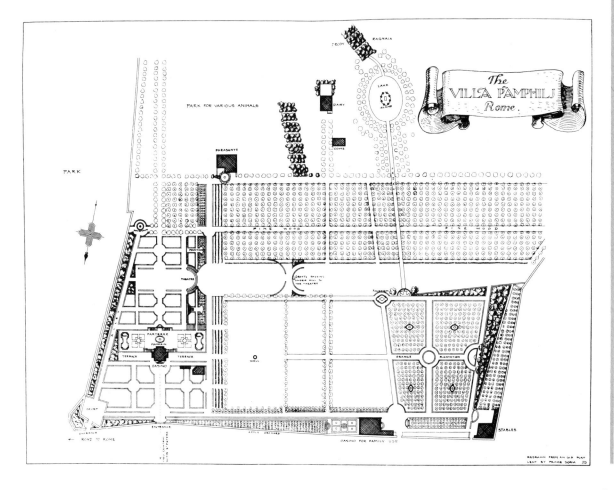

The Roman climate does not favour lawns. Consequently, the 'English' park, which replaced Algardi's lower parterre garden, is a desolate sight. Perhaps the grass would look better if it was mown. At present it grows in a series of alternately tufty and balding patches. The sunken pit of the amphitheatre can still be seen, however the niches in its semicircular wall are bare, and it is adorned only by Pamphili lilies and swags of *spugne*.

Algardi's grotto, which is set into the hillside between the casino and the amphitheatre, has recently been restored. There is an ornate nineteenth-century fountain at the centre of the lower garden. Its marble bowl is supported by satyrs carrying baskets of fruit on their heads.

It is important to remember that the casino and its gardens represent a very small part of the park, which once had a circumference of almost 6 miles. Wooded slopes extend to the south and west, giving way above the casino to a large area of level ground that was used as a *manège*. Below the trees that bound the *manège* there is a short canal. A series of rustic cascades descend from the fountain of the lily to a small lake. This area was laid out at the end of the seventeenth century, when the shores of the lake were used as a small hunting reserve. Today, the canal teems with tame coypu, who come out onto the banks to be fed cold pasta and banana skins by passing children.

A copy of Bernini's beautiful Fountain of the Queen, better known as the *Lumaca*, or snail, stands in the meadow above the canal. Olimpia Pamphili is said to have persuaded Innocent X that it was too small for its intended setting in Piazza Navona.

The family villa lies on the road that forms the park's northern boundary. The walls still stand around what remains of Algardi's orange grove. Valvassori's Fountain of the Tiber is set into the wall opposite the villa. The air of desolation that haunts the park is especially concentrated in this corner.

Villa Doria Pamphili	
Nearest major town:	Rome
Advance booking:	No
Owner:	Commune
Address:	Via San Pancrazio
Location:	The entrance to the park lies just beyond the Porta San Pancrazio. There is a small, unattended carpark at the junction between Via San Pancrazio and Via Aurelia Antica. The casino is a ten-minute walk from the carpark. The no. 41 bus goes to Porta San Pancrazio, and nos 44 and 710 go along the Via San Pancrazio.
Open:	Dawn–dusk
Admission:	Free. Casino not open to the public
Wheelchairs:	Yes, with assistance
Refreshments:	No
Lavatories:	No

Previous page: Villa Doria Pamphili. The Art of Garden Design in Italy, Triggs, 1906. (Bodleian, 19187 b.6.)

Right: Villa Doria Pamphili: the parterre garden.

IL QUIRINALE

NINETEENTH-CENTURY GARDEN • SOME SIXTEENTH-CENTURY FEATURES

HISTORY

During the fifteenth century, Cardinal Carafa built a small villa on his family land on the Quirinal hill known at the time as Monte Cavallo. In 1550 it was rented by Cardinal Ippolito d'Este. He had been frustrated in his papal ambitions, but was still in need of a Roman residence while he considered the development of his future home at Tivoli. The first garden on the site was laid out between 1550 and 1554 by Girolamo da Carpi. In 1560 Pius IV gave the cardinal an adjoining estate, and he began to extend both villa and garden.

In 1572 Ippolito died, and the property passed to his nephew Luigi d'Este. He preferred spending his time at Tivoli and offered the use of the villa to the new Pope, Gregory XIII. The Pope was enthusiastic about the situation, later described by Evelyn as 'most excellent for ayre and prospect'. The open and still rural hill was a far healthier place than the low-lying area by the Tiber. He made substantial alterations to the villa and also increased the water supply to the gardens.

In 1585 Gregory died, leaving a request that the improved property should be returned to Luigi d'Este. Instead, his successor, Sixtus V, bought the land from the Carafa, who were still the landlords. He had the villa enlarged yet again, by Domenico Fontana. Subsequent popes transformed the villa into the palazzo that we see today. Several architects were employed, including Maderno and Bernini. The great Organ Fountain beneath the palazzo was built by Giovanni Fontana in 1596.

By 1670 the garden was laid out as about 60 square parterres with intersecting avenues of cypress. This rather monotonous plan survived largely unaltered until the nineteenth century, when the great central avenue was cut through the grounds. The delightful summerhouse was added in 1741.

From the time of Sixtus onwards, the palazzo became the principal papal residence and was occupied by 29 popes. Of this number 22 died there. Curiously, each in turn bequeathed his heart and viscera to the church of SS Vincent and Anastasius. In 1870 the property was forcibly taken over by the kingdom of Italy, and now serves as the presidential palace.

Il Quirinale: the Fountain of Venus.

Il Quirinale	
Nearest major town:	Rome
Advance booking:	Yes
Owner:	The State
Address:	Via del Quirinale, Roma
Location:	In the centre of the city. Buses nos 71/81/415 run past it. The garden entrance is in the Via del Quirinale.
Open:	By arrangement with Dott. Battisteri, Direttore dei Giardini del Quirinale, Tel: 06–4699–2526. Permission normally given only to visitors with a special interest in the gardens.
Admission:	Free
Wheelchairs:	Yes
Refreshments:	No
Lavatories:	Yes

THE GARDEN

The gardens can roughly be divided into two areas, the 'English' garden and the *giardino all'italiana*. It is still possible to trace some of the sixteenth–century layout of the latter garden, although it has been radically transformed by its many owners. It is entered through what was once the stable block. Once past the magnificent presidential guards (not a man under six foot six tall), you find yourself between the two gardens. They were divided by lawns and a wide gravel path with a central fountain. This was laid out during the nineteenth century, under the care of Gregory XVI. The finest of the garden's many palm trees grow in this area, some dating back to 1736. Unfortunately, several of them succumbed to the bitter winter of 1985.

On either side of the garden there are immense hedges of bay and laurel. These were being pruned during our visit, and the air was filled with the scent of bay. The pruning was being done by an army of men wielding long-handled billhooks, which have been found to produce a healthier hedge than more modern methods. Ten years ago many of the hedges were in a very poor state, and the director of the garden had them lowered by nine feet. They have responded extremely well.

Behind the hedges are a number of ilexes of enormous age, several of which are known to have been planted during the tenure of Ippolito d'Este. On the right is the 'English' garden, planted with palms and maritime pines. Flower-filled Roman sarcophagi line the paths. At the centre is a superb plane tree, claimed to be the oldest in Italy.

The *giardino all'italiana* lies to the left. Here, as elsewhere, the hedges surrounding the repetitive square parterres of the seventeenth–century garden have grown to enormous heights. They have been left to form a fascinating and mysterious set of interconnected garden 'rooms'. Each has stone benches, where you can sit in deep shade while gazing at the square of blue sky above you. Arches cut through the hedges give sudden exciting glimpses of statues and fountains. It is unlikely that many visitors to the Quirinal Palace have played hide-and-seek here, which is a sadly wasted opportunity. An avenue through the centre of this area is lined with *commedia dell'arte* figures, including one of a cobbler using his shoe to separate two quarrelling pigs.

Beyond this garden lies the delightful summerhouse, or coffee-house. This was built in 1741 for the meeting of Pope Benedict XIV and Charles III of the Two Sicilies. Classical busts line the roof, while others stand on tall columns in front of it. The Fountain of Venus is in front of

PROSPETTIVA DEL GIARDINO PONTIFICIO SVL QVIRINALE. *Architettura di Ottavio Mascarini.*

the coffee-house and, unusually for Italy, there is also a handsome sundial. This one is said to have been designed by Borromini for Urban VIII in 1628. The base bears the Cybo crest. A garden 'room' to the right of the coffee-house contains a rustic fountain with spouting dolphins and stone turtles. *Giochi d'acqua* spurt up on all sides, enclosing the victim in a ring of spray. At the far end of the garden is the maze, added during the last century.

There is a raised terrace at the right-hand end of the palace. From here you can look down at the enormous grotto containing the Organ Fountain. This is currently undergoing a long-awaited restoration. It was originally prepared in 1565 to contain Apollo and the Muses. The hydraulic organ was added in 1596. A recess to one side has a life-size figure of Vulcan at his forge, with Cupid working the bellows.

Left: *Il Quirinale*. Ville e giardini di Roma, *Falda, 1683.*

Above: *Il Quirinale: the summerhouse.*

Following the transition from monarchy to republic, there was a lengthy period during which the gardens were not developed. Now, however, they are being beautifully maintained by a staff of fourteen. The present director recognises that it would be pointless to attempt a return to the Renaissance layout. He is seeking to restore the gardens to their early nineteenth–century appearance.

GIARDINI VATICANI

PAPAL GARDENS • BEAUTIFUL SIXTEENTH-CENTURY CASINO

HISTORY

It was not until the Middle Ages that the Vatican became the permanent home of the papacy. The fourth–century basilica of St Peter stood in open countryside until Leo IV enclosed it. His fortifications were built between 848 and 852, and during the thirteenth century the first palace was built near the basilica. The first references to a garden date from this time; lawns and an orchard are mentioned. There was also a herb garden.

Following the return of the papacy from Avignon in 1377, major changes began to take place. The fifteenth century saw the completion of the palace, the construction of the Sistine Chapel and the proposals for the rebuilding of St Peter's. More important for the history of gardens, it also saw the construction of the Villa Belvedere (also known as the Palazzetto). This was built by Innocent VIII in 1485. It stood on a hill just outside the Leonine walls to the north of St Peter's. The villa, turning its back firmly on the Vatican, was used as a retreat by the Pope, who suffered from very poor health.

Innocent's court was dominated by the powerful figure of Cardinal Giuliano della Rovere, already described as 'Pope and more than Pope'. As soon as he was elected, as Julius II in 1503, he began the greatest building programme the Vatican had yet seen. The most famous of his works is, of course, the rebuilding of St Peter's. However, he was a great collector of antiquities, and had a fondness for the Villa Belvedere. In 1504 he commissioned Bramante to produce a design that would link the palace to the villa, and enable the latter to be used to display his collection of statues.

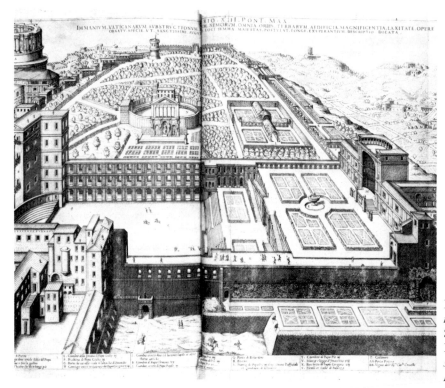

Left: *Giardini Vaticani: the Cortile del Belvedere.* Speculum Romanae Magnificentiae, *Lafreri, sixteenth century. (British Library, C. 77.i.11)*

Above: *Giardini Vaticani:
the* giardino all'italiana.

The area between the two buildings consisted of about a ¼ of a mile of rising ground. Bramante's solution was to enclose the ground by extending wings from each end of the palace towards the villa. The resulting rectangular space was known as the *Cortile del Belvedere*. A balustraded walk (the *Stradone*) ran along the top of each wing. The lowest area was an arena overlooked by a stepped amphitheatre beneath the façade of the palace. Half-way along, a series of ramps and terraces ran between the two wings. These provided additional seating for spectators, as well as giving access to a large formal garden at the top. At the far end of this garden the rectangle was completed by a two-storey loggia running from side to side. The focus of the whole conception was provided by a great exedra in the centre of the loggia. The villa remained a private place on the far side of the loggia, the space between the two buildings becoming a

courtyard where Julius's statues could be displayed. This courtyard was greatly altered in the eighteenth century, but must have been most beautiful. It was planted with a grove of orange trees and filled with fountains. Julius wished his collection to be open to the public, and so Bramante's famous spiral staircase was built to create public access to the courtyard without the necessity of entering through the palace.

This magnificently imaginative garden no longer exists. We make no apologies for describing it at some length, for it and its successor, Villa Madama, created an entirely new way of thinking about garden landscapes. The Belvedere courtyard, with its lavish use of fountains and deliberate placing of

Giardini Vaticani: the casino of Pius IV.

sculpture, was a harking back to Roman antiquity and a model for all subsequent Italian gardens.

In 1585 the Vatican library was built across the middle of the garden, destroying its proportions. Later the Braccio Nuovo (part of the museum) was also built across the garden, resulting in the loss of the terraces. The *Cortile del Belvedere* now refers only to the lower courtyard, used as a carpark. The formal upper garden has become a dull expanse of grass called the *Cortile della Pigna*. They can both be seen while visiting the Vatican museums, but it is perhaps best just to look at contemporary engravings of the garden at its peak.

There is another Vatican building of great importance in the context of gardens. This is the casino of Pius IV, or Villa Pia. It was begun in 1558 by Pirro Ligorio for Paul IV, who died soon after its commencement. It was completed under the Medici Pius IV, who took particular pleasure in it.

The subsequent history of these gardens is one of constant change, as each incumbent in turn left his mark. With the creation of the Vatican State in 1929 a great deal of building took place. One loss which occurred was the Square Garden. This lay to the west of the *Cortile della Pigna*. It had originally been created, during the 1540s, as a secret garden for Paul III. It was walled and held four square parterres divided by *berceaux*.

THE GARDEN

In order to visit these gardens it is, sadly, no longer necessary to obtain a letter of introduction from a cardinal and then to have it franked by the Vatican major-domo. However, ease of entry perhaps compensates for a little vanished romance. Space does not allow us to compete with the excellent and comprehensive official guidebook, so we shall restrict this description to the major features of the garden.

The tour begins by following the *Viale dell'Osservatorio* through the most recently laid-out section of the grounds. It winds up the hill to the Leonine walls, which, until 1929, marked the limit of the gardens. The central tower was built in 848 for defence against the Saracens, and withstood a French siege a thousand years later. Below the Broadcasting Centre is the *giardino all'italiana*, with two simple fountains and box parterres. It replaces the vanished Square Garden. The *giardino all'inglese*, at the northern end of the walls, is in the form of an attractive oak wood filled with fountains. Beyond this is the *Fontana dell'Aquilone* (great eagle). Its impressive flow of water comes by way of Trajan's ancient aqueduct from Lake Braccione, 20 miles away. The aqueduct was restored by Paul V and the fountain was built in 1611 by the Dutch architect Van Santen (Giovanni Vansanzio) to commemorate the restoration. The water flows from here through many other fountains, culminating in St Peter's Square. The eagle and the water-spouting dragons are references to Paul V's Borghese crest.

From the fountain you walk down the slope to the casino of Pius IV. The grace and charm of this perfect garden retreat are almost matchless. Its only possible equal is the casino at Caprarola, which it predates by nearly 25 years. It houses the Papal Academy of Science, and special permission is needed to see the interior (enquire at the ticket-office).

It takes the form of a small casino and an open loggia which face each other across an oval courtyard. Both structures are richly decorated with stucco reliefs, mosaic and frescoes. It was built at a time when a sincere Christian faith went hand-in-hand with an open-minded Renaissance humanism. This is reflected by the use of scenes from classical mythology for exterior decoration, and of religious imagery for the interior. This happy balance did not last long; in 1569 the reforming Pius V disposed of nearly all the classical statues which decorated the casino. (He also banished visitors from the fine collection of statues in the Belvedere.)

The parterres that once radiated from the casino have long gone. There is now a small eighteenth-century sunken piazza to the east. This gives a marvellous view of the loggia rising from the pool at its feet. The piazza is filled with the sound of water flowing into the pool on either side of the loggia. Above the water sits an ancient statue of Cybele. The gay mosaic panels on either side of her, though not original, are perfectly in keeping with the spirit of the building. They replace four stucco caryatids, removed during a nineteenth-century restoration. The work was probably done by the Vatican School of Mosaic, whose building stands in the grounds.

Giardini Vaticani	
Nearest major town:	Rome
Advance booking:	No, but see below
Owner:	Vatican State
Location:	The ticket-office is close to St Peter's (on the left as you face the church). For the Cortile del Belvedere, entrance as for the Vatican museums, about ½ a mile round the Vatican walls to the right.
Open:	Tue, Thur, Sat: guided tours at 10.00. Vatican museums daily 9–1. (NB: it may not always be possible to enter the Cortile della Pigna and the Cortile del Belvedere. They can be seen from the museum windows.)
Admission:	L9000, museums L8000
Wheelchairs:	Yes
Refreshments:	Yes
Lavatories:	Yes

CAMPANIA

Campania is the most southerly of the regions covered by this book. It is mostly low-lying and is extremely fertile. Under Roman rule it earned the reputation of being an earthly paradise; its beautiful coast was lined with magnificent villas and gardens. In the towns the houses were built around smaller, domestic gardens, similar to those that can still be seen in Pompeii.

During the eleventh century southern Italy was conquered by the Normans. Although they destroyed the beautiful Sicilian pleasure gardens of their Muslim predecessors, later, when building gardens themselves, they chose to adopt the Islamic style. This tradition was brought to Naples and the mainland by Emperor Frederick II in the thirteenth century. He had grown up in the court at Palermo, and he built gardens around his castles throughout southern Italy.

Royal gardens continued to be laid out in Campania throughout the fourteenth and fifteenth centuries. Those at Poggio Reale were designed at the end of the fifteenth century for the Crown Prince of Naples. They so impressed Charles VIII of France that he took a Neapolitan gardener home with him to design Italian gardens at Amboise and Blois.

Villa Cimbrone: the terrace.

LA REGGIA

EIGHTEENTH–CENTURY ROYAL GARDEN IN CENTRAL CASERTA

HISTORY

In 1734 Carlo III became the first Bourbon ruler of the Kingdom of the Two Sicilies. He was a great huntsman, and used to ride out from Naples to the woods of Caserta. He became so fond of the place that he eventually decided that it should be transformed into the new capital of his kingdom. He expelled the Caetani, who had been its rulers, and in 1751 he commissioned Luigi Vanvitelli to draw up plans for a new town, a gargantuan palace and a garden.

By the end of 1751, Vanvitelli had already set to work on staking out an extension to the existing *barco*. In 1756 he published his plans under the title of *Dichiarazione dei Disegni del Real Palazzo di Caserta*. The area immediately in front of the palace was to be laid out as a series of enormous *parterres de broderie*, while the rest of the garden was to be divided up between a series of garden 'rooms', decorated with fountains. There was to be a pool with a circular island, an orchard and a gazebo on the crest of the hill opposite the palace. The plans show Carlo's hunting wood, intersected by a series of wide rides, and included in the layout of the garden.

Very little of the original plan for Caserta was realised. In 1759 Carlo III left Italy to become King of Spain, and made over his Italian possessions to his eight-year-old son Ferdinando. Vanvitelli continued to work, but his attention was devoted largely to the palace and to the problem of finding sufficient water for the garden. The aqueduct that he had begun in 1753 was finally completed in 1762. It brought water to the site over a distance of 20 miles. In 1770 he turned his attention to the garden once more, but three years later he died.

Carlo Vanvitelli took over after his father's death, and it is to him that the garden should rightly be attributed. In 1777 the canal was excavated and the embankments were built for the ramps that enclose the Fountain of Juno. Turf seeded in the royal cowsheds was laid down to either side of the canal the following year. In 1782

Vanvitelli worked with an Englishman called John Graefer to design the 'English' garden that lies to the east of the Fountain of Diana. (Graefer later laid out Nelson's garden at Castello di Maniace in Sicily.)

In 1838 De Lillo was employed to lay out a flower garden and a *manège* to the right of the palace. The area in front of the building was left untouched, as by this time open lawns were far more fashionable than Vanvitelli's elaborate *parterres de broderie*. Work on the gardens continued until 1860, when the property passed to the House of Savoy. During the events that surrounded the unification of Italy the palace was plundered, and for many years the gardens were neglected.

THE GARDEN

The gardens at Caserta were part of a massive and unrealised plan by which the royal palace was to be linked to Naples. An avenue flanked by canals was to be laid out along the route of the ancient Via Appia. A section of the road was completed before Carlo III's departure for Spain, but the plan was soon abandoned. However, something of the effect that Vanvitelli intended to achieve can be appreciated from the grotto at the top of the water staircase. The straight line of the canal gives way to a road which continues through the massive portico of the palace and stretches beyond it to the horizon.

Carlo Vanvitelli's canal is punctuated by sculpted scenes from Ovid's *Metamorphoses*, and divided by shallow cascades. The layout represents a gradual progression from the cultivated to the wild, and culminates in the rough-hewn water staircase that climbs the hill almost 2 miles from the palace.

If grandeur could be achieved by scale alone, then Vanvitelli's aim would have been realised. However, the absence of any real sense of proportion reduces the impact of the vast garden. The groves of ilex and camphor that stand to each side of the canal deprive it of the width that might

La Reggia: Venus and Adonis.

have served to balance its enormous length. The sculptures, which should represent the climax of the design, dwindle into insignificance, and are virtually invisible from the windows of the palace.

After its 20 mile journey through pipes and aqueducts, the water, on which the garden relies for its effect, is released at the top of the water staircase. Luigi Vanvitelli intended that it should eventually pass under the palace and emerge in the two canals that were to flank the Via Appia to

Naples. A foaming cascade pours down the staircase, creating a dramatic background for Paolo Persico's vivid sculptures of Diana and Actaeon. The unfortunate huntsman has just been turned into a stag. His dogs crowd around him in confusion and Diana, surrounded by her nymphs, looks across the water from the safety of her own island.

The water from the Fountain of Diana disappears underground below the pool and then re-emerges to form the long basin of the Fountain of

Venus. Gaetano Salamone executed the figures of Venus and her nymphs bidding farewell to Adonis, in 1780. One of the nymphs is playing with Adonis' hunting dog, and the wild boar that is destined to kill him appears to be waiting expectantly. The heads of other wild animals adorn the pool from end to end.

Beyond the fountain the water disappears underground again, to emerge beneath Ceres and her court. It also flows to either side of the goddess from the upturned amphorae of two tritons. Ceres' bronze wheat sheaf disappeared long ago, but the putto that sits to one side of her still holds a medallion displaying the Trinacria, which is the emblem of Sicily. The pool is divided by another water staircase, and the shallow steps are decorated with a series of different faces.

Once again the water disappears. This time it is spanned by the road at a point known as the Bridge of Hercules. It emerges as a magnificent cascade which descends into the Fountain of Juno and Aeolus. The semicircular fountain represents the climax of the garden. The sculptures were executed by Angelo Brunelli, Andrea Violani, Persico and Salamone. Juno was to have sat in the middle of the great pool, in a carriage drawn by peacocks. Aeolus is at the centre of the scene, sitting with his back to the Palace of the Winds. The winds themselves, newly released, writhe and squirm on the rocks to either side of him. Bas-reliefs set above four of the arched doorways of the 'palace' represent Jupiter and the goddesses, the marriage of Thetis and Peleus, the judgement of Paris, and the marriage of Paris and Helen. The fountain is enclosed by two curving ramps decorated with statues.

The financial constraints that prevented the completion of the Juno Fountain also made their mark on the Fountain of the Dolphins. The three dolphins that spit water into the final pool are very modest by comparison with the extravagant compositions of the other fountains. Beyond their pool the road stretches away towards the palace, interrupted only by the simple Fontana Margherita, which is decorated only with a basket of flowers.

The grand *peschiera* lies to the west of the central axis, on a level with the Dolphin Fountain. Ferdinand IV's little retreat, known as the *Castellucio*, is also to be found in this area.

La Reggia	
Nearest major town:	Caserta
Advance booking:	No
Owner:	The State
Address:	La Reggia
Location:	The palace lies in the centre of Caserta, on the left-hand side as you enter from Rome. (NB: a bus runs the length of the garden every 30 minutes.)
Open:	Jan, Feb 9–2.30, Palace 9–1.30
	Mar 9–3.30, Palace 9–1.30
	Apr 9–4.30, Palace 9–1.30
	May 9–5.30 Palace 9–1.30
	Jun–Sept 9–6, Palace 9–1.30
	Oct 9–4.30 Palace 9–1.30
	Nov 9–3.30, Palace 9–1.30
	Dec 9–2.30 Palace 9–1.30
Admission:	Garden L2000 Palace L3000
Wheelchairs:	Yes
Refreshments:	Yes
Lavatories:	Yes

La Reggia: the view down the garden's central axis.

VILLA CIMBRONE

TWENTIETH-CENTURY VILLA AND GARDEN IN SPECTACULAR COASTAL POSITION

HISTORY

At first glance Villa Cimbrone appears to be a fortified medieval palace, built in the same Moorish style as the courtyard at Villa Rufolo. It may come as a surprise to learn that the villa and garden were both created during this century. The land on which they stand was bought in 1904 by an Englishman called Ernest Beckett, who was soon to take the title of Lord Grimthorpe. He is said to have paid 100 lira for a ruined farmhouse, a wood, a walnut grove, a vineyard and a magnificent view over the Gulf of Salerno.

Grimthorpe chose not to employ a qualified architect. Instead, he enlisted the help of a local tailor called Nicola Mansi, with whom he spent the next fifteen years in creating the villa and its garden.

He died in 1917, two years after its completion.

In 1915 Grimthorpe's sister bought the land below the belvedere and employed Mansi to build a smaller house for her family. The little villa was called the *'Rondinaia'*, or 'swallow's nest', and for many years it was the home of Gore Vidal.

Villa Cimbrone stayed in the family until 1960, when it was sold to its present owner by Grimthorpe's daughter. Marco Willeumier had

Below: *Villa Cimbrone.*

Right: *Villa Cimbrone: the terrace.*

Villa Cimbrone

Nearest major town:	Ravello
Advance booking:	No
Owner:	Signor Marco Willeumier
Address:	Via S. Chiara 26
Location:	Well signposted from the centre of Ravello. Can only be reached on foot. It is a steep climb, and there are several flights of steps.
Open:	Winter, 8.30–5 Summer, 8.30–8
Admission:	L2000
Wheelchairs:	No
Refreshments:	Yes
Lavatories:	Yes

known Lord Grimthorpe and his family for many years, and they were most anxious that he should take it over. The beautiful condition of the garden today serves as ample explanation for their anxiety. Willeumier's grandfather came to Ravello from Switzerland. He opened the Palombo, which was the first hotel on the Amalfi coast. It is still owned by the family, and Marco Willeumier has extended the business by opening part of Villa Cimbrone to guests.

THE GARDEN

Visitors to Villa Cimbrone must find their way through the backstreets of Ravello to an impressive 'medieval' portal, apparently built to withstand cannon balls and battering rams alike. A little door set into the massive structure of the gate leads directly into the garden. The shady courtyard of the villa lies to the left, and beyond it there are steps leading down to the crypt.

The garden is surrounded by terraced hillsides, and Lord Grimthorpe seems to have felt no temptation to impose this traditional form upon the sloping site of his garden. He was content to divide it simply between a lower and upper garden and an area of wooded hillside intersected by winding paths. Each level was built to frame a different aspect of the magnificent view.

On entering, one's eye is drawn at once along a straight walk leading from the villa to a magnificent terrace overlooking the sea. It is flanked by ornate walls, shaded in part by a pergola of vines, and spanned by a bridge that links the two levels of the garden. Beyond the walk a circular belvedere shelters a statue of Ceres, silhouetted against the sea. The terrace is perched 1000 feet above the sea, which seems to stretch to infinity beyond the classical busts that adorn the wall.

A winding path leads down the hill behind the terrace and into the oak and chestnut woods. There is a 'neoclassical' building, known as the Temple of Bacchus, built on a ledge below the terrace. The bronze figure of Bacchus is a copy of a well-known classical statue, which can be seen in the Civic Museum in Naples. Lord Grimthorpe's ashes are buried beneath it.

A natural cave further down the hillside contains an eighteenth–century statue of Eve. Its rugged walls create a striking setting for her pale figure.

Villa Cimbrone.

The upper garden may be reached from the woods by way of the fine cypress avenue that leads to the rose garden. While the sea forms a background for the lower garden, this area is designed to frame the impressive peaks of the mountains. It is bounded by a line of maritime pines, and divided into two distinct areas by a decorative wall. The inner garden, which is enclosed by the wall, is filled with beds of roses set out around a sundial. The outer garden provides a setting for a series of classical figures – made to appear authentic by the effects of wind and weather. A seat set into the far wall bears a quotation from the 'Rubaiyat of Omar Khayyam'.

Between the rose garden and the villa there is a charming summerhouse, built in the same style as the villa and decorated with colourful tiles. It stands in a lovely secret garden, which is filled with a regular pattern of beds laid out around an eighteenth-century fountain. A curious collection of twentieth-century bronzes and mock-medieval columns stands in front of the summerhouse.

VILLA RUFOLO

THIRTEENTH-CENTURY MOORISH COURTYARD GARDEN IN CENTRAL RAVELLO

HISTORY

Villa Rufolo was built by the wealthy Rufolo princes of the thirteenth century. The family's prosperity originally derived from trade. Their ships travelled all over the Mediterranean, and their principal imports were luxurious goods from the East.

The Rufolo reached the height of their splendour when they became bankers to Carlo I, the Angevin king who ruled Naples between 1266 and 1285. By the beginning of the fifteenth century, however, the family had died out, but a fragment of their garden survives, representing a precious relic of the period during which Islamic tradition shaped the gardens of Naples and Sicily.

Between the fifteenth and seventeenth centuries, the palace belonged to the Confalone and Muscettola families. In the eighteenth century it passed to the d'Afflitto, whose renovation of the villa destroyed some of its original features.

In 1851 a Scottish botanist called Francis Neville Reid bought Villa Rufolo and entrusted its restoration to Michele Ruggiero, who was supervising the excavations at Pompeii at the time. Reid created the modern garden that is laid out between the medieval buildings, and the find terrace that overlooks the sea.

In 1974 the property was bought by the local tourist board. A small museum was established in 1982.

THE GARDEN

Villa Rufolo commands a view of the Gulf of Salerno. It has two towers: one that served as a lookout, and another that was an ornamental addition to the gateway marking the entrance to the garden. This is flanked by two fierce crocodiles. Two more monsters look down on the entrance to the courtyard. Their gaping mouths once served to extinguish the flaming torches of guests before they entered the palace.

The courtyard consists of a colonnade surmounted by a delightful loggia. Slender columns are arranged in pairs to either side of the loggia's elaborate arches. The wall above is decorated with Moorish arabesques. Unfortunately, its beauty is somewhat marred by the massive buttresses that were inserted after it was badly damaged by storms in 1713.

Originally, pots of orange trees, lemon trees and flowering plants adorned the garden. The air was cooled by a central fountain, and the colonnade offered deep pools of shade. This idyllic place would have been unimaginable in the castles of central or northern Italy.

The rest of the garden dates from the nineteenth century and is laid out on two levels. The open loggia that overlooks the sea on the lower level, is thought to have served as an al fresco dining room.

Villa Rufolo	
Nearest major town:	Ravello
Advance booking:	No
Owner:	The State
Address:	Piazza del Duomo, Ravello
Location:	Entrance on the piazza in the centre of Ravello.
Open:	9.30–1, 2–4.30
Admission:	L1000
Wheelchairs:	Yes, for courtyard only
Refreshments:	No
Lavatories:	No

CHRONOLOGICAL TABLE

Year	Campania	Emilia	Lazio	Liguria	Lombardy	Marche	Piedmont	Tuscany	Veneto
1250	P. Rufolo								
1458								V. Medici P. Piccolomini	
1495		Il Moro							
1504			Vatican						
1519			V. Madama						
1522						V. Imperiale			
1530					Il Bozzolo				
1538								Castello	
1547									V. Torre
1549								Boboli	
1550			Quirinale					Gamberaia	
1552			Bomarzo						
1555			V.d'Este						
1559			P. Farnese						
1560		Marfisa							
1564				P. Tursi					
1565									Giusti
1566			V. Lante						
1568					V.d'Este				
1570									Cataio
1580								Leonini Vicobello	Marcello
1589								Petraia	
1592					V. Cicogna				
1598			Aldobrandini						
1615							Agliè		
1617			V. Borghese						
1620								de'Gori	

Year	Campania	Emilia	Lazio	Liguria	Lombardy	Marche	Piedmont	Tuscany	Veneto
1632							Is. Bella		
1640			Pamphili						
1650								Torrigiani V. Reale	
1652								Garzoni	
1656									Allegri
1669									Barbarigo
1680								Cetinale	
1690					V. Carlotta				
1697							P. Reale		
1720						Buonaccorsi			
1722									Trissino
1735									Pisani
1738								Corsi-Salv.	
1756	Caserta								
1763						Caprile			
1775									Prato d.V
1780								Geggiano	
1783									Rizzardi
1837				Durazzo					
1867				La Mortola					
1880				Negrotta					
1903							San Remigio		
1904	Cimbrone							La Pietra	
1908								I Tatti	
1922			Ninfa						
1938								Giullarine	
1950								Arrighetti	

BIOGRAPHICAL NOTES ON ARTISTS

Aleotti, Gian Battista, 1546–1636
Architect from Parma. Worked in Parma and Ferrara.

Alessi, Galeazzo, 1512–72
Leading Genoese architect. Born in Perugia, trained in Rome, where influenced by Michelangelo. Worked in Genoa and Milan.

Algardi, Alessandro, 1602–54
Sculptor, decorator, architect. Trained in Bologna, active in Venice, Mantua, Rome and Naples.

Ammanati, Bartolomeo, 1511–92
Architect and sculptor. Born in Florence, trained by Bandinelli. Worked in Venice, Padua, Rome and Florence.

Bandinelli, Baccio, 1493–1560
Florentine sculptor much influenced by Michelangelo.

Bernini, Pietro, 1562–1629
Florentine sculptor. Worked in Naples and Rome. Father of Gian Lorenzo Bernini.

Bonazza, Giovanni, active 1695–1730
Venetian sculptor.

Borromini, Francesco, 1559–1667
Brilliantly original, if eccentric, Baroque architect. Born in Lombardy, worked principally in Rome.

Bramante, Danato, 1444–1514
One of the greatest Renaissance architects. Influenced by Leonardo da Vinci. Born in Urbino, worked principally in Rome.

Buontalenti, Bernado Timante, 1536–1608
Mannerist architect, sculptor and painter working in Tuscany.

Cassetti, Giacomo, 1682–1757
Venetian sculptor. Trained under Grazio Marinali.

Cerrato, Domenico, 1715–92
Architect from Vicenza working mainly in Padua.

Collino, Filippo, 1737–?
Piedmontese sculptor working for the House of Savoy.

Collino, Ignazio, 1724–93
Piedmontese sculptor working for the House of Savoy.

Da Udine, Giovanni, 1487–1564
Decorative artist, studied under Raphael.

Dal Pozzo, Girolamo, 1718–1800
Veronese architect.

Fontana, Carlo, 1638–1714
Architect working mainly in Rome. Trained under Bernini.

Fontana, Giovanni,
Hydraulic engineer. Worked mainly in and around Rome.

Frigimelica, Girolamo, 1653–1732
Venetian architect.

Genga, Girolamo, 1476–1551
Painter and architect from Urbino. Influenced by Raphael.

Giambologna (Giovanni da Bologna), 1529–1608
Mannerist architect and sculptor. Trained in Antwerp, worked mainly in Florence.

Le Nôtre, André, 1613–1700
Famous French gardener. His best known work is at Versailles and Vaux-le-Vicomte.

Ligorio, Pirro, 1510–83
Painter, architect and archaeologist. Born in Naples, worked mostly in Rome.

Maderno, Carlo, 1556–1629
Architect. Born in Lombardy, worked in Rome.

Marchionni, Carlo, 1702–86
Roman architect.

Marchiori, Giovanni, 1696–1778
Sculptor working in Venice.

Marinali, Orazio, 1643–1720
Venetian baroque sculptor.

Michelozzi, Michelozzo, 1396–1472
Florentine architect, sculptor and decorator. Worked for Cosimo the Elder.

Muttoni, Francesco, ?–1748
Venetian architect.

Peruzzi, Baldassare, 1481–1536
Sienese architect and painter. Worked mostly in Rome, with Bramante and Raphael.

Pinsent, Cecil, 1884–1964
English architect and landscape designer. Worked in England, Italy and Yugoslavia.

Porta, Giacomo della, 1537–1602
Lombard mannerist architect, follower of Michelangelo.

Rainaldi, Girolamo, 1570–1655
Roman architect.

Raphael (Raffaello Sanzio), 1483–1520
Painter and architect, born in Urbino. From 1508 worked in Rome. Perhaps the greatest Renaissance artist in the classical style.

Ripamonte, Riccardo, 1849–1930
Milanese sculptor.

Romano, Giulio, 1492–1546
Mannerist architect and painter. Assistant to Raphael, also influenced by Michelangelo.

Rossetti, Biagio, 1447–1516
Born in Bologna. Planner and architect to the Ferrarese court.

Sangallo, Antonio da (the Younger), 1485–1546
Roman architect. Born in Florence. Trained under Bramante and Peruzzi, assistant to Raphael.

Scamozzi, Vincenzo, 1552–1616
Venetian architect.

Tacca, Pietro, 1577–1640
Florentine sculptor, worked in Florence and Livorno.

Tibaldi, Pellegrino (Il Pellegrini), 1527–96
Lombard architect and painter. Worked in Rome, Milan and Spain.

Tirali, Andrea, 1660–1737
Venetian baroque architect and sculptor.

Tribolo (pseudonym of Nicolo Pericoli), 1485–1550
Florentine sculptor and engineer.

Valvassori, Gabriele, 1683–1750
Roman architect.

Vansanzio, Giovanni, ?–1622
Known as Il Fiammingo. Flemish architect working in Rome.

Vanvitelli, Luigi, 1700–73
Neapolitan architect. Worked in Rome, Naples and Ancona.

Vignola, Giacomo Barozzi da, 1507–73
Leading Roman architect. Studied at Bologna, worked with Ammanati. Influential writings on architecture.

Vittoria, Alessandro, 1525–1608
Venetian sculptor. Influenced by Giovanni da Udine.

GLOSSARY

automata hydraulically powered human or animal figures, designed to move, spout water or play musical instruments.

berceau an arched pergola or tunnel supporting climbing plants such as vines.

bosco (pl **boschi**) a wooded area enclosed within a garden. It owes its origins to the 'sacred grove' of the Greeks and the Romans, and provided the essential touch of wildness in the otherwise ordered world of the garden.

caryatid sculptured female figure used as a supporting column.

giardino all'italiana garden in the Italian style. Usually a formal arrangement of box parterres, often arranged around a fountain.

giardino segreto secret garden. Originally a small area enclosed for privacy; later a major feature of many gardens.

giochi d'acqua 'water games'. Concealed sprays designed to surprise the onlooker.

herm a garden ornament consisting of a three-quarter–length figure on a pedestal.

limonaia a shelter for overwintering potted citrus trees. Sometimes referred to as a 'stanzone'.

manège an open space for riding practice.

nymphaeum in classical gardens, a shrine or grotto with fountains dedicated to the nymphs.

palazzina small villa.

parterre a flowerbed laid out in a regular manner.

parterre de broderie a bed laid out with an elaborate flowing pattern often formed from clipped box (broderie/embroidery).

peschiera fishpool.

piano nobile the principal floor of a house, usually the first floor.

putto (pl **putti**) cupid or cherub.

quincunx a grove of trees planted in regular arrangements of fives; typically, one at each corner of a square and one in the centre.

ragnaia (pl **ragnaie**) bird snare made out of nets covered in bird lime and stretched between the branches of trees.

rocaille elaborate decoration made up of rock-like forms, shells and scrolls.

spugne rough texturing of grotto walls in imitation of coral.

tapis vert a (usually rectangular) stretch of grass.

term a tapering pedestal bearing a bust. They were used as boundary markers in the ancient world.

BIBLIOGRAPHY

Acton, Harold, *Tuscan Villas*, Thames and Hudson, 1973

Chigiotti, Giuseppe, 'The Design and Realization of the Park of The Royal Palace at Caserta by Luigi and Carlo Vanvitelli', in *Journal of Garden History*, Vol 5, No. 2, Apr–Jun 1985

Coffin, David R., *The Villa in the Life of Renaissance Rome*, Princeton, 1979

Coffin, David R., *The Villa d'Este at Tivoli*, Princeton, 1960

Darnall, M. and Weil, M., 'Il Sacro Bosco di Bomarzo: Its sixteenth century literary and antiquarian context', in *Journal of Garden History*, Vol. 4, No. 1, Jan–Mar 1984

Hibbert, Christopher, *The Rise and Fall of the House of Medici*, Penguin, 1979

Jellicoe, Goode and Lancaster, *The Oxford Companion to Gardens*, OUP, 1986

Lees–Milne, Alvide, 'Ninfa: a garden in the ruins of a town', in *Hortus* 5, 1988, pp. 40–49

Lodari, Renata and Carola, 'Villa San Remigio a Pallanza', I *Quaderni* 1, Museo del Paesaggio, Verbania

Masson, Georgina, *Italian Gardens*, Thames and Hudson, 1961

Phillips, E.M. and Bolton, E.T., *The Gardens of Italy*, London, 1919

Shepherd, J.C. and Jellicoe, G.A., *Italian Gardens of the Renaissance*, London, 1925

Tagliolini, Alessandro, *Storia del giardino italiano*, Usher, 1988

Triggs, Harry Inigo, *The Art of Garden Design In Italy*, London, 1906

Veneto, Regione del, *Il Giardino Veneto*, Electa, 1988

Visentina, M.A., 'La Grotta nel cinquecento veneto: il Giardino Giusti di Verona', in *Arte Veneta Annata* XXXIX

Wharton, Edith, *Italian Villas and their Gardens*, New York, 1904

INDEX